PERSPECTIVES ON INDIAN SOCIETY AND HISTORY: A CRITIQUE

Perspectives on Indian Society and History: A Critique

Edited by

HETUKAR JHA

MANOHAR
2002

First published 2002

ISBN 81-7304-422-8

Published by
Ajay Kumar Jain for
Manohar Publishers & Distributors
4753/23 Ansari Road, Daryaganj
New Delhi 110 002

Typeset by
Kohli Print
Delhi 110 051

Printed at
Rajkamal Electric Press
Delhi 110 033

Contents

Contents

Contributors

SABYASACHI BHATTACHARYA, Professor of History, Centre for Historical Studies, Jawaharlal Nehru University; former Vice-Chancellor, Visva-Bharati University, Shantiniketan.

BINAY BHUSHAN CHAUDHURI, former Professor and Head, Department of History, University of Calcutta, Calcutta.

SURENDRA GOPAL, former Professor and Head, Department of History, Patna University, Patna.

HETUKAR JHA, Professor of Sociology, Patna University, Patna.

RAMKRISHNA MUKHERJEE, Director, Centre for the Appraisal of Social Reality and Quality of Life, Calcutta; former 'Distinguished Scientist', Indian Statistical Institute, Calcutta.

K.S. SINGH, former Director-General, Anthropological Survey of India, New Delhi.

Introduction

Hetukar Jha

The social sciences and history have a fairly long and vibrant tradition in India. Systematic and thoughtful probes into the complexities of life and living conditions are constantly made from the different perspectives of these disciplines. However, it seems to be quite desirable that such perspectives should be periodically subjected to critical appraisal in order to assess their validity and relevance. This exercise involves the task of scrutinizing the significance and efficacy of the 'concepts' held crucial in the discourses of these disciplines. These concepts form part of the battery of tools used for exploration, understanding, explanation and interpretation of social and historical facts. The way such concepts are understood and used reflects their underlying perspectives that implicitly or explicitly guide the perception of socio-historical reality. A critical examination of these concepts may, therefore, reveal the status of the perspectives incorporating them in terms of their capacity of comprehension and appropriateness. This volume is chiefly devoted to this task and presents the contributions of distinguished social scientists and historians with insightful discussions and analysis of 'caste', 'class', 'tribe', their inter-relationship, and of 'region' as well as the approach of 'regional history'.

Ramkrishna Mukherjee draws the attention of social scientists to the issues of 'caste in itself', 'caste and class', and 'caste in class', and briefly discusses each in terms of its appropriateness in the historical context. He describes the emergence of the cultural interpretation of the caste system since colonial days. According to him, it was Max Weber who had denounced Marx's contention regarding the caste system as a system denoting the relations of production in ancient and medieval periods. After independence, Weberian notion gained ground and is, at present, the dominant perspective. But, the approach of 'caste in itself', that follows Weberian idea, does not appropriately depict the Indian reality. Class structure has cut across the caste heirarchy giving rise to 'new alliances and antagonisms'. Under the circumstances, Mukherjee suggests that 'caste in class' appears to be the appropriate approach to understanding Indian social reality today.

Binay Bhushan Chaudhuri elaborates on caste-tribe contact in the eastern part of India as observed by administrators of the colonial period and anthropologists such as Sarat Chandra Roy, Martin Orans, Nirmal Kumar Bose and Surajit Sinha. His focus is on the tribal communities of Bhumij, Santal, Munda, Oraon and Ho, which had linkages with their non-tribal neighbours, and, therefore, were not 'primitive isolates'. An exchange of cultural traits between them must have occurred under the circumstances. However, Chaudhuri's main objective in this context is to examine the validity of 'Hinduization' of tribes.

He analyses the works of H.H. Risley, W.W. Hunter and various official records of the British period regarding the socio-religious and political movements of tribal communities. He also closely examines the historical and anthropological studies of such movements. He contends that differential diffusion characterized the spread of Hindu influence among the tribes. Those who became known as 'Rajputs' were averse to the idea that their entire community should follow their example and become Rajputs like them. So, the bulk of the community remained separate from the Hindufold. This *segmentary integration and assimilation*, an important phenomenon of Indian history and anthropology, is intensively discussed by Chaudhuri. His analysis can facilitate in explaining the present day *tribe versus dikku* relationship within the tribal zone and the relationship between tribal and non-tribal leaders in the arena of state and national level politics.

Sabyasachi Bhattacharya deals with the issue of regional history in the context of theoretical development of the discipline of history in India. He discusses the relevance of the identification of 'region', and suggests that it is a product of history. A historian/ social scientist should use a concept of region appropriate to the theme of his/her research. According to him, regional history 'allows us to explore details of the interplay between economic, social and cultural factors. . . . We need to explain big things.' It also helps in developing a history of the 'historyless common man'. Bhattacharya throws light on the process of the construction of 'region' by historians and discusses the role of the emergence of consciousness of regional identity in this context. He also points out the role of history in promoting such consciousness. However, he cautions against undertaking the approach of regional history in an isolationist or narrow view. It should not remain divorced from the broader, national frame.

Surendra Gopal contends that regional history free from an isolationist or circumscribed view affords much insight and import for national history. In this context, he describes the peasant protest movements against indigo planters which began in north Bihar in the 1860s. The movement first began in Pandoul (in the present district of Madhubani) in north-eastern Bihar. Initially it was a local affair, but it soon influenced the peasants of Champaran in north-west Bihar. The issue, then, became a matter of regional concern. Further, as Gandhi joined it, it became tagged with national history. Gopal systematically discusses the linkage of the local with the regional and that of the latter with the national which significantly contributes to the understanding of the dynamics of history.

K.S. Singh analyses Jyotirishwara's *Varna Ratnakara*, an early fourteenth century work that contributes not only to the knowledge of regional history, but also throws light on pan Indian trends and approaches in the middle age. Composed in Maithili prose, this work is based on the author's observations of socio-political life and his knowledge of Sanskrit literary tradition. *Varna Ratnakara* qualifies to be, perhaps, the first survey document of north India containing rich ethnographic data and a first hand account of the quality of urban life at that time. Singh focuses on the ethnographic materials and analyses their significance for understanding pan Indian conditions prevalent at that time. Soon after independence, an eminent intellectual had made an appeal that sociologists and anthropologists of India should study Indian traditions, that is, broadly, Indian history, for developing Indian sociology and anthropology. Following this point of view, Singh analyses a document of regional tradition and finds its contents meaningful in the context of knowledge regarding the people of India as a whole.

All these five papers are revised versions of the lectures delivered at Darbhanga in Bihar. About a decade ago, Kam Sundari Devi (also known as Kalyani Devi), the surviving wife of the last Maharaja of Darbhanga, Kameshwar Singh, set up a foundation for the promotion of socio-cultural and educational activities at Darbhanga. One such activity of this foundation, known as Maharajadhiraja Kameshwar Singh Kalyani Foundation, is to organize lectures of eminent intellectuals at Darbhanga. Thus, Ramkrishna Mukherjee, K.S. Singh and Binay Bhushan Chaudhuri were invited to deliver lectures in 1996. In the following year Sabyasachi Bhattacharya and Surendra Gopal gave lectures. All these scholars graciously agreed to travel to a distant town and communicate their ideas to an audience representing the intelligentsia of a large part of north-eastern Bihar. It is hoped that the local intelligentsia would have gained at least some idea of the issues affecting seriously the course of social sciences and history today. Credit, however, goes to these scholars for this diffusion and dissemination of knowledge. Besides, it is hoped that the lectures published in this volume would be considered by social scientists and historians of the country as invaluable to their pursuit.

'Caste in Itself', 'Caste and Class', or 'Caste in Class':

A Brief Discussion of the Three Concepts in the Historical and Contemporary Perspectives in India

Ramkrishna Mukherjee

After the British conquered Bengal and eventually the whole of India, they set out to administer the colony. In this context they encountered two phenomena with which they were not familiar: (1) the relation of people to land for production (and not for revenue receiving, household living, etc.), and (2) the caste system of India, viz., the *jati* stratification of society.

Soon they realized that the varna stratification of society (which denotes the varnas of Brahman—mainly priests, Kshatriya—the warriors, Vaisya—the husbandmen, and Sudra—the lowly people) is not unique to Indian society. In the late nineteenth and early twentieth century, J. Jolly, H. Oldenberg, E. Senart and others clarified that the varnas denote the status system in Hindu society, which (e.g. varnas) are found with different nomenclatures in other societies of the world.[1] This point I have discussed in my book *The Dynamics of a Rural Society*.[2]

Yet, in 1962, M.N. Srinivas[3] rediscovered the distinction between varna and *jati*, and, in 1995, A. Beteille[4] endorsed this 'pathbreaking essay' of Srinivas at the All-India Sociological Conference in Bhopal. However, that *jatis* denote the caste system of India was universally acclaimed; namely, the smallest endogamous groups of people within each varna.

The relation of Indian people to land for production (and the ancillary activities of trade and petty craft production) did not, at first, undergo this kind of confusion. British researchers observed in the eighteenth-nineteenth centuries that the instruments for production (viz., plough, cattle, seed, manure) were held by the Indians familywise, but land for production was held by the villagers in common under the village community system. As later admitted by Lord Bentinck,[5] this unified strength of the Indian peasants, artisans, and traders under the village community system was undermined following the introduction of the zamindari system. This system was first introduced in 1793 in Bengal, Bihar and Orissa (the *subah* of Bengal) as the Permanent Settlement of Land, and in due course spread all over India.

Some European scholars in the late twentieth century argued that the manorial system was present in India from the early times of pre-British India, and that the village community system is a myth. However, the falsification of history in this manner has not been accepted by the large community of scholars.

They have documented that the village community system had originated at the threshold of the last millennium or some centuries earlier, and flourished up to the eleventh century AD. The steady but slow growth of indigenous capitalism in India, tried to undermine the village community system, especially during the Mughal period, and ventured upon establishing the manorial system. This point was first mentioned by D.D. Kosambi[6] and, later, elaborated by Irfan Habib and others. However, such was the gravity of the village community system that it could not be uprooted by indigenous capitalism; indeed, it slowed down the capitalist development of India because the latter could not penetrate village India and create a home market. The point was underscored as late as the middle of the twentieth century by the Congress Agrarian Reforms Committee in its *Report* of 1951 (All India Congress Committee, New Delhi).

However, the falsification of the role of the caste (*jati*) system in India took a distinctive turn beginning with the research on the caste system by British scholars in the eighteenth-nineteenth centuries and most of the Indian scholars swallowed the myth hook, line, and sinker.

In my aforementioned book and in *The Rise and Fall of the East India Company*,[7] I have shown that the *jati* division of society denoted the relation of people to land for production and the ancillary artisanal and trading activities. The *jatis* proliferated along with specialization and division of labour in society; but movements against the *jati* system gathered momentum along with the advent of capitalism in Indian society on its own merit. This point has been elaborated by later scholars.

I have discussed, especially in *The Dynamics of a Rural Society*, that the caste system received a new lease of life by invaginating itself into the colonial class system ushered in by the colonialists. Moreover, I have discussed in *The Rise and Fall of the East India Company*[8] that the anti-caste movements of the fourteenth-seventeenth centuries were suppressed by the British by enacting laws supporting the Hindu and the Muslim orthodoxies from the time of Warren Hastings in India (1772–86). But this real history of India was distorted by British scholars, and the large majority of Indian scholars followed suit.

The *jati* division of society was viewed in the realm of 'cultural' relations, viz., interdining, intermarriage, purity-pollution, and other such customary behaviour and perception. The fact that in British India landlords, big landowners, wholesale traders, moneylenders, etc., belonged essentially to the high castes was overlooked, as was the fact that the majority of self-sufficient peasants, small-scale artisans, petty traders, etc., belonged to the middle castes in general. Those at the lowest echelon of the growing colonial-capitalist class structure (e.g. marginal peasants and landless workers), belonged overwhelmingly to the lowest castes and 'Tribes'. This is how the caste structure had invaginated itself into the class structure evolved in colonial India.

Doubtless, all high caste people did not comprise the highest echelon of the growing class structure, just as all the middle castes did not constitute the middle echelon of the class structure, and all lowly castes did not belong to the lowest echelon of the class structure. But an overview of Hindu society substantiated this correlation between the caste and the capitalist class structures.[9] Contrariwise, the view that was ideologically imposed by those who hailed the British rule in India is that the caste structure ruled society.

Max Weber denounced the fact that the caste system denoted the relations of production and property in ancient and medieval India by proclaiming that it was a product of 'Brahamanical theodicy'. In his own words:[10]

All factors important for the development of the caste system operated singly elsewhere in the world. Only in India, however, did they operate conjointly under specific Indian conditions: the conditions of a conquered territory within ineffable, sharp, 'racial' antagonisms made socially visible by skin colour. . . . [This] well-integrated, unique social system could not have originated or at least could not have conquered and lasted without the pervasive and all powerful influence of the Brahmins. It must have existed as a finished idea long before it conquered even the greater part of North India. The combination of caste legitimacy with *karma* doctrine, thus with the specific Brahmanical theodicy—in its way a stroke of genius—plainly is the construction of rational ethical thought and not the production of any economic 'condition'.

As opposed to this 'cultural' interpretation of *caste in itself*, Karl Marx had written earlier:[11]

The primitive forms of property dissolve into the relations of property to the different objective elements conditioning production; they are the economic basis of different forms of community, and in turn presupposes specific forms of community. These forms are significantly modified once labour itself is placed among the *objective conditions of production* as in slavery and serfdom.

[Where] the particular kind of labour—*i.e.* its craft mastery and consequently property in the instruments of labour—equals property in the conditions of production, this admittedly excludes slavery and serfdom. However, it may lead to *an analogous negative development in the form of a caste system.* (emphasis added)

Marx's formulation of *caste for class* under specific feudal conditions was stoutly rejected by Weber who, however, had misconceived caste by his formulation of 'Brahmanical theodicy' to denote merely the varna stratification of society. Later Indianists following Weber extended the formulation *caste in itself* to the *jati* stratification of society. In this respect, Louis Dumont[12] raised the misconception to an Olympian height by declaring the uniqueness of caste-ridden Indian people as Homo Hierarchicus. The general run of Western scholars and the great majority of Indian scholars, led by M.N. Srinivas, supported and propagated the perception that caste *sans* class represented 'modern' India. Sanskritization and Westernization were proclaimed to be the vehicles for ushering in 'social change in modern India'.[13]

A false consciousness was thus generated in India, and spread in society. No wonder that a political scientist wrote in the *Reader's Digest* in 1950 that caste is in the Indian blood!

Meanwhile, the inexorable course of capitalism, doubtless colonial in character, was spreading in India. From the 1920s, in particular, land and crops began to be transformed into commodities from their subsistence character. Alienation of land and accumulation of crops enriched some (though not many) peasants, artisans and traders who were placed low or still lower in the caste hierarchy. Now, in comformity with their enhanced economic status, they aspired for a better 'social' status. A new alignment between caste and class was in the offing, in place of the caste structure merely invaginating itself into the class structure of society.

This alignment was viewed by national chauvinists, as a variant of the decolonized modernizers upholding the view of *caste in itself*, as the interaction of two discrete entities, caste and class; class being imported by the Raj and not displaying itself from immemorial times as *caste for class*—in the view of Marx. N.K. Bose[14] portrayed the structure of Hindu society in terms of caste division, and Andre Beteille[15] elaborated the thesis by clearly writing on *caste, class and power.*

Caste and class became a catchy formulation to denote the social structure of Indian society. However, with its ideological ('cultural') commitment it soon merged itself into the formulation of *caste in itself* and employed the same idioms as Sanskritization and Westernization to denote 'social change in modern India'.

Meanwhile, colonial capitalism and later, the independent

Indian capitalist system, had their impact on the invagination of *jatis* into the capitalist social structure. In the last days of the Raj, the 'Depressed Classes' clamoured for equality in economic and cultural perception and behaviour with the 'high castes', and the Raj pacified them by enacting the Scheduled Castes Order in the 1930s, in order to consolidate their own political position in society. After independence in 1947, the Indian leaders retained the nomenclature of the Scheduled Castes, and added that of the Scheduled Tribes, although, by this time, there were no tribes as undifferentiated (or little differentiated) groups of people even in the remote areas of India.[16] Later, the government further categorized the 'Other Backward Classes' in order to make the new *avatar* of caste hierarchy complete; namely, the high castes, Other Backward Classes, the Scheduled Castes, and the Scheduled Tribes.

Yet, the social processes heralding the triumph of class structure over caste hierarchy could not be altogether ignored by the avatar makers of caste. But they obfuscated reality. M.N. Srinivas mooted the notion of 'Dominant Caste' in the 1960s, in which caste was in the appellation and not in content. His identification of a 'Dominant Caste' had six attributes;[17] (1) 'sizeable amount of the arable land locally available', (2) 'strength of numbers', (3) 'high place in the local hierarchy', (4) 'western education', (5) 'jobs in the administration', and (6) 'urban sources of income'. All these attributes are secondary or tertiary expressions of the formation of the top stratum of the class structure in rural society. But the proclamation of class relations was an anathema to these conservative scholars. So, class was forcibly funnelled into an amorphous identity of the 'Dominant Caste' because as later admitted by its progenitor, all these six attributes need not be present in one caste entity. In other words, the 'Dominant Caste' could be identified in $(2^6-1) = 63$ ways!

The result was that the devout young scholars were duly brainwashed to search for the 'Dominant Caste' in different societal segments in various ways, and even assert the dominant *class* character of the identified 'Dominant Caste'! For example, in Jehanabad district of Bihar the landless agriculturists of low castes have organized themselves to secure a better deal from the big landowners—the Bhumihar Brahmins, while the landowners have retaliated ruthlessly. They have even formed a paramilitary force by the name of Ranvir Sena which regularly organizes massacres of the landless families. The government hardly takes any action on this issue, while some enthusiastic academics search for the role of the 'dominant caste' at this junction in society. Instances like this in Maharashtra, Madhya Pradesh and other states have aggravated the confusion of the 'caste ridden' society, which provides succour to the role of the caste system in present-day India.

Today, casteization of society is proceeding at the level of *hoch politik* with the help of some academics. At the other extreme, at the level of *neben politik*, caste is denoted more and more as an identification *within* the class stratum its constituents belong to. This is similar to the distinction drawn between the Jews and the Gentile, or the ethnic groups, within the class structure of the USA, Britain, etc.

Indeed, the reinforced false consciousness, generated by scholars and politicians alike, has been so pervasive in the upper political level that even in relatively recent times the Mandal Commission earmarked caste as the criterion of backwardness in Indian society. M.N. Srinivas and other scholars were party to enforcing the false consciousness of Indian social reality. From the academia, I.P. Desai's was the lone voice to castigate this manner of falsification of social reality. In a seminal article,[18] he emphasized that the criterion of 'backwardness' should be sought in the class relations in modern India. But his voice was smothered by the dominant scholars and politicians.

In the meantime, reality asserted itself at the grassroots level. The correlation between caste and class in colonial India is being transformed into 'caste in class'. The Scheduled Castes and Scheduled Tribes—not to speak of the Other Backward Classes—are ranged within the spectrum of the high, middle, and low echelons of the class system in society. This is clearly manifested in the political alliances among these categories.

Also in 'cultural' matters, the differentiation is growingly manifest within the evolved class categories of the Scheduled Castes and 'Tribes', such as even among the Santals, Oraons and Mundas of Bengal, Sabaras of Orissa and Bengal. In this respect, I found from a quality of life study in 1980 in Delhi and its environs that the upper echelon of the Scheduled Castes were aspiring for 'cultural' equality with the upper echelon of the high castes. Speaking at a seminar at the Department of Sociology, Jawaharlal Nehru University in 1997, K.L. Sharma[19] said that he had observed in his study of a number of villages in Rajasthan over a period of 10 years that the 'upper' Scheduled Castes were inviting the upper echelon of the 'high castes' to their life-cycle ceremonies like marriage, and the latter were readily participating in these ceremonies.

On the other hand, rumblings of discontent are heard within the monolithic constructions of the lowly castes; such as, of the Dalits (literally, the downtrodden). M.V. Nadkarni[20] has shown that in the southern parts of Tamil Nadu the 'weaker' sections of the Dalits are raising their voice against the usurping 'stronger' segment of the Dalits. Such discontent is not unheard of in Maharashtra, Gujarat, and even in Bihar (as among the Santals and Oraon-Mundas).

Thus, it is that we should not look at caste as a 'new avatar' as scholars have recently proclaimed, Class structure has cut across the caste hierarchy, forming new alliances and antagonisms. Indeed, it is in the process of withering away along with the march of history or it remains as an atavism, like the distinction between the Jews and the Gentile, the Hindus and Muslims. Yet, it is propped up, for their own gain by politicians and a brand of social scientists. Today in India, *caste in class* depicts the reality, and not caste *per se* or *caste and class*.

NOTES

1. See J. Jolly, 'Beitrage *Zur* indische Rechtgeschichte', *Zeitschrift der Deutschen Morgen Iandischen Gesellscraft*, Leipzig, Band 50, 1896; H. Oldenberg,'Zur Geschichte des indischen Kastenwesen', *Zeitschrift*

der Deutschen Morgenlandischen/Gesellscaft, Leipzig, Band 51,1897; E. Senart, *Les Castes dans'* l'Inde, Paris: Librarie Orientaliste Paul Geuthner, 1927.

2. See R. Mukherjee, *The Dynamics of a Rural Society*, Berlin: Akademie Verlag, 1957.
3. M.N. Srinivas, *Caste in Modern India and Other Essays*, Bombay: Asia Publishing House, 1962, pp. 63–9.
4. A. Beteille, 'Varna and Jati', *Sociological Bulletin*, vol. 45, 1, 1996, p. 16.
5. See Lord William Bentinck, 'The Speech on November 8, 1829', in A.B. Keith, *Speeches and Documents on Indian Policy: 1750–1921*, vol. l, Cambridge: Cambridge University Press, p. 215.
6. See D.D. Kosambi, 'The Basis of India's History (1)', *Journal of the American Oriental Society*, vol. 75, 1, 1995.
7. R. Mukherjee, *The Rise and Fall of the East India Company*, Berlin: Verlag der Wissenscaften, 1957, pp. 140–212; rpt., New York and London: Monthly Review Press, 1974.
8. Ibid., pp. 313–35.
9. Mukherjee, *The Dynamics of a Rural Society*, pp. 1–58.
10. M. Weber, *The Religion of India*, Glencoe: The Free Press, 1958, p. 131.
11. K. Marx, *Pre-Capitalist Economic Formations*, London: Lawrence & Wishart, 1964, pp. 101–2.
12. See Louis Dumont, *Homo Hierarchicus*, Paris: Gallimard, 1966.
13. See M.N. Srinivas, *Social Change in Modern India*, Bombay: Allied Publishers, 1966.
14. See N.K. Bose, *Hindu Samajer Garan*, Calcutta: Visva-Bharati, 1949 (in Bengali), English translation by A. Beteille, *The Structure of Hindu Society*, New Delhi: Orient Longman, 1976.
15. See A. Beteille, *Caste, Class and Power: Changing Patterns of Stratification in a Tanjore Village*, Berkeley: University of California, Bombay: Oxford University Press, 1966.
16. See P.K. Bose, *Classes and Class Relations among Tribals of Bengal*, New Delhi: Ajanta Publications, 1985.
17. Srinivas, *Social Change in Modern India*, pp. 10–11.
18. I.P. Desai, 'Should "Caste" be the Basis for Recognizing Backwardness?', *Economic and Political Weekly*, vol. 19, 28, 1984, pp. 1106–16.
19. K.L. Sharma, *Social Stratification in India: Issues and Themes*, New Delhi: Sage, 1997.
20. M.V. Nadkarni, 'Broadbasing Process in India and Dalits', *Economic and Political Weekly*, vol. 32–4, 1997, pp. 2160–71.

Society and Culture of the Tribal World in Colonial Eastern India:

Reconsidering the Notion of 'Hinduization' of Tribes

Binay Bhushan Chaudhuri

This paper addresses the question of characterizing the growing Hindu–Adivasi culture contacts in colonial eastern India. The primary concern here is to understand the nature of Hindu influence on the adivasi world. Recently, scholars have argued that the culture contact was not merely a unidirectional movement, i.e. Hindu ideas influencing adivasis all the time, and have pointed out the simultaneous existence of a reverse process, calling it 'tribalization'. Only a brief reference will be made to it, since it will be argued, as a phenomenon of culture contact it was far less significant during the period under study.

The major question that will be discussed here and my central argument in this regard is: To what extent is the usual concept 'from tribe to caste' a valid characterization of the nature of Hindu cultural influence on the tribal world? This will be examined with reference to the adivasi communities of Bhumij, Santal, Munda, Oraon and Ho.

The concept 'from tribe to caste' did not have the same meaning for all the contemporary observers–bureaucrats of the colonial administration and the Christian missionaries, and later, the professional anthropologists. A term often used by the bureaucrats to describe the increasing Hindu influence on the adivasis is 'Hinduization'. By this, they sometimes mean emulation by the adivasis of some Hindu cultural traits—religious beliefs, rituals and practices. 'Hinduization' in this restricted sense may have occurred without involving any tribe—caste continuum. Typically, however, they used the term to denote an increasing intergration of the tribal world in the caste-based Hindu social organization, so much so that the tribes ceased to exist as separate entities. As will be discussed, the official perception in this regard evolved over time. In fact, it was in terms of this concept that the colonial administration partly tried to understand the rise and growth of the radical tribal agrarian movements since about the mid-nineteenth century. The official perception seems to have first crystallized into a coherent form in the writings of Risley (1891) and others. In his study of the changing adivasi society and culture, Risley particularly observed those instances where the growing Hindu influence led to a complete effacement of the old tribal identity.[1] He emphatically asserted in 1915, 'All over India at the present moment tribes are gradually and insensibly being transformed into castes'.[2] Anthropologists, too, seldom doubted the occurrence of the process, though they held different views on its extent. In general, they do not agree with Ghurye's view postulating a near completion of the process of transition from tribe to caste. In central India, he believed, the 'so-called' aborigines were actually 'Hindu subcastes', 'backward Hindus', differing only in degree from the other segments of Hindu society.[3] Most anthropologists, however, would not go as far, and regarded Hinduization as a gradual, steady and incomplete process. Nirmal Kumar Bose's exposition of his concept, 'the Hindu method of tribal absorption',[4] suggests that the process was long drawn one. Moreover, as Bose argued, the 'Hindu method' was unique in that it did necessitate a complete obliteration of the tribal culture. Its numerous traits did survive the Hinduization process. Surajit Sinha and others elaborated 'the mechanisms by which distinct social and cultural identities are maintained'.[5]

It will be argued that the question 'from tribe to caste' may be differently viewed and also that the available evidence does not quite support at least some of the representations of the tribe-caste 'movement'. A brief statement of the central argument is as follows. Since tribal societies were not, admittedly, 'primitive isolates' at all, and often closely interacted with the material and non-material cultures of their neighbours, emulation by both of each other's cultural traits naturally occurred. Evidently, the adivasis came under the Hindu influence in the process. This, however, did not invariably necessitate their articulation with the caste-based, hierarchical Hindu social organization, or even with the specific economic organization prevailing in the 'Hindu' neighbourhood. More importantly, the usual representations of the 'Hinduization' process ignored the will and the subjectivity of the adivasi communities emulating the Hindu cultural influences. Since this subjectivity is a crucial aspect of this process of emulation, there is a need to identify its major determinants. Some relevant questions need to be answered. Why did the adivasis respond to the Hindu influences in the way they did? Why did they choose only some aspects of the Hindu culture rather than the others? Was this responsiveness identical in nature throughout, or, was it particularly noticeable during certain periods of their history? Did the adivasi world as a whole identically respond to Hindu influences, or, did the response significantly vary from group to group? All this suggests that the so-called movement from tribe to caste was far more complex than its usual representations normally assumed. Anthropologists, though aware of such complexities, did not accommodate all of them in their analysis. For instance, they wrote of the adoption by tribals of devices toward maintaining their identity. The question they failed to answer is why the tribals were simultaneously keen on emulating Hindu traits and preserving their own identity. It also remains an open question if the exposure of tribals to Hindu material and non-material culture would necessarily lead to their integration in the Hindu social organization. Its occurrence was conditional on the nature of the countervailing process, i.e. the strength of the adivasi efforts to preserve their own identity. The integration was easier where the opposite force was non-existent or weak.

Before discussing the empirical part of the study, i.e. the changing representations of the Hinduization process and the 'tribe–caste continuum', a brief examination of the reverse process called 'tribalization',[6] is in order. This would serve to show that Hinduization and tribalization were far from two parallel cultural processes of an identical qualitative value. Tribalization was a far weaker force, and the background of the two processes was strikingly different. K.S. Singh defined the 'traditional aspect' of tribalization as 'acceptance of tribal mores, rituals and beliefs by incoming communities'. He went as far as to call it a 'countervaling process' in relation to Hinduization. Singh's own description of the process in some tribal areas of Bihar clearly revealed that its social base was extremely narrow. The 'acceptance of tribal mores, rituals and beliefs by incoming communities' did not, affect the 'Brahmins and other high-caste people'; the communities actually influenced were generally 'other categories of castes who with their background of animistic belief did not encounter any difficulty in being assimilated into the cultural world of the tribe'.[7] Singh concluded: 'In fact it seems that acceptance of tribal mores was easier for the middle and lower segments of the caste hierarchical order who moved in search of land or to offer their services, and artisans who served their tribal masters.' Two other aspects of tribalization noted by Singh were 'respect for the tribal priest and medicine men and for tribal deities which was retained even after the tribals were driven out of the village', and 'the tribals' participation in the formation of the state [the Nagbansi Raj in the Munda country of Chotanagpur] and their continued support for it'. An extract cited by Singh from the *District Gazetteer, Hazaribagh* describes the first:

> Even where the landlord and the majority of the tenants are Hindus it is still the custom to employ as *pahan* or sacrificer one of the race of the original clearers of the village, or at least, of an earlier dispossessed race. The idea underlying this is a belief in the existence of local spirits who must be propitiated by sacrifices, lest their anger vent itself on the fruits of the fields and cattle and the fertility of the women, or in the stirring up of disease for men and beasts.[8]

It is not clear from this description whether the tribals had completely deserted the village in which such a 'belief' survived, or despite their degraded status continued to stay on their land which had been appropriated by 'Hindu' tenants. Had the supposition that the *pahan's* 'brethren have long been expelled' been true, then why should have Hindu intruders ('the Brahmin or Babhan grantee or purchaser of a jungle village') been wary of abandoning the old practice of sacrifices for propitiating the 'local spirits'? The continuing role of the *pahan* as a sacrificer made sense only if the alleged 'expulsion' of tribals had been partial. Nevertheless, propitiation of revengeful gods capable otherwise of making mischief was not necessarily a distinctive trait of the tribal culture. On the other hand, the 'tribals' participation in the formation of the state' and the 'high ritual status offered by the rulers to them' need not be regarded as a typical instance of 'tribalization'. Their participation was presumably restricted to a negligible number of Munda families. The practice had lost all real meaning in the context of the growing resentment of Munda villages towards the Nagbansi royal family and its various dependents. The so-called tribalization in the Munda country and also elsewhere was a far weaker force than Hinduization, and it is going too far to call it a 'countervailing process' in relation to Hinduization. The cruical factor in this weakness was the conscious manner in which the hierarchical Hindu caste society distanced itself from the tribal community because of a complex about its cultural superiority. This is evident from the low ritual ranking of the tribal groups where they were admitted at all into the caste system. In general, they remained outside its pale. Buchanan Hamilton's description of the utterly disdainful attitude of the caste Hindus to ward Santal immigrants in Bhagalpur and Birbhum in the first decade of the nineteenth century is revealing. Perceived as a source of pollution, the Santals were not even allowed to milk the cows of upper caste Hindus. Buchanan also noted that any violation of the norm created a stir in the village. However, a curious observation made by him was the caution on the part of the local Hindus not to antagonize the Santals. He attributed this to their practice of witchcraft, Hindus were fearful of 'black magic' which they perceived as a source of potential harm to them. The well-known skill of the Santals as waste reclaimers was perhaps another reason why they were tolerated by Hindu landlords.[9]

One will now focus on the central concern of this paper: understanding the nature of Hindu influence on the adivasi world during the colonial period. Professional anthropologists have systematically dealt with this theme. The bureaucrats of the colonial administration also offered useful information and insight. After tracing the process chronologically, the discussion will be on the changing representations of the phenomenon of the increasing Hindu influence on the adivasis. This will be followed by an examination of the views of some leading anthropologists in this regard.

Buchanan's *Bhagalpur Journal* may be regarded as one of the first descriptions by a bureaucrat of the life of an adivasi community, the Santal, in the Hindu cultural milieu of Bhagalpur and Birbhum. The description points to the isolation of the two communities—Hindu and Santal. He noted the disdainful attitude of the caste Hindus toward the Santal immigrants in these districts, the Santals were perceived as a source of pollution. On the other hand, an elaborate report (1833) on the origins and nature of the Bhumij revolt (1832–3) described the numerous Bhumij tribe, particularly of Burrabhum, Dhalbhum and Manbhum, as a largely Hinduized group.[10] The relevant part of the report will be cited here and comments on the limitations of the process will be made while examining the empirical basis of the so-called Hinduization.

> The chief portion of the inhabitants of Burrabhum are Bhoomijes with a small number of Kormies and Sonthals and other low castes and a slight sprinkling of Brahmins, Rajpoots, Bania traders and Mahomedans. . . . With regard to the manner of the Bhoomijes, they are rather a turbulent and refractory race. . . . They are short in stature, stout, muscular and not unlike their neighbours the Coles (Kols), with whom they intermarry, thus affording reasonable grounds for deducing them from a common origin. I am scarcely qualified to speak of their religion. They profess to be Hindus of the Brahminical persuasion, but no respectable Brahmin will officiate for them. They have no temples or buildings for their religious ceremonies. But a large tree or clump of trees is selected for this purpose near the

village under which a stone is placed in the ground, and a little red paint smeared on it which is called the *Burroo* (name of the God) *Ka Than* [*Buru Ka Than* meaning the place of worship of Buru, the supreme God]. The Nya who is the headman of the village officiates at their festivals, of which there are three principal ones in each year. The chief of these is the Sarool Pooja which takes place in Bysakh [April–May], previous to commencing their grain. They are celebrated with feasting and dancing, both men and women joining in the latter diversion. They have in general left off eating cow's flesh, which their Cole brethren indulge in, but still use the flesh of fowls and sheep as food. . . . They first burn their dead and collect their bones and bury them marking the place by a stone. The language is the Bengalee, but I have never met with [sic] a Bhoomij in Burrabhum, who could read or write it. To the westward, adjoining Singbhum, the people also speak Tar, the language of the Coles.

The report reveals the considerable degree of exposure of the Bhumij to Hindu cultural influence and also points to the limitations of the so-called Hinduization process, which is evident from the persistence of old tribal beliefs and institutions. Two striking instances of 'Hindu' influence were the abandonment of cow flesh and the large-scale substitution of the Mundari language by Bengali. Only cow flesh was given up, not the flesh of fowls and sheep. Bengali was largely used as the spoken language. The fact that only rarely could the Bhumij read and write Bengali does not make the change any less significant. However, vital elements of the old culture survived the obvious Hindu influence, which contradicted the claim of the Bhumij 'to be Hindus of the Brahminical persuasion'. There were quite a few crucial instances of survival. No 'respectable Brahmin' agreed to 'officiate' for the Bhumij. Only the traditional priest of the tribal village (*Nya, Naike*) presided over their religious ceremonies. Unlike the Hindus, the Bhumij did not have any 'temples or buildings' as places of worship. For their worship they continued to gather at the old 'sacred grove' of the village—the shade of a tree or a clump of trees. Burying the bones of the dead, regardless of the place of death, in the native village, a stone (*isasandiri*) marking the burial spot, was a distinctively Munda custom. Later reports on Hindu influence on adivasi societies noted a differential diffusion of the influence, the degree of emulation of Hindu traits varied with the social and economic status of the different adivasi groups. The report cited here does not mention anything of the kind.

A contemporary account of the Munda revolt (1831–2), known as the Kol revolt, suggests that the Hinduization process was far more limited in the Munda-Oraon country. While explaining the widespread rebellion against some members of the royal family, the Nagbansi Raj, the local administration analysed the implications of its increasing inclination to Hinduism in terms of the composition of the 'bureaucracy' of the Munda state and the control of various aliens, including brahmins, over a large number of Munda villages. The Hindu influence was evidently largely confined to the royal family. Originally belonging to the tribal group itself, it had never taken any initiative in promoting Hindu culture among the Mundas. Nor did they themselves show any interest, except in isolated cases, in the religion of the royal family, about which they were increasingly bitter.

The elaborate account of the first Santal revolt (1855) did not refer to any notable Hindu influence. As will be discussed later, the religious rituals which the leader, Sidhu, asked his followers to practise punctiliously, revealed the influence of the Hindu notion of purity. The Santal society was probably familiar by then with the idioms of Hindu faith and religious rituals. The rapid spread of Hindu influence since about the beginning of the Santal Kherwar movement (1874) indicated that the ground for it had already been partly laid. The influence did not yet take any distinct institutional form. This explains why two contemporary works on the Santal—E.G. Mann's, *Sonthalia and the Sonthals* (1867) and W.W. Hunter's, *The Annals of Rural Bengal* (1868) completely ignored Hindu influence on the Santal culture, material and non-material. In fact, Mann was particularly struck by the Santal consciousness of an identity despite their dispersion over a large geographical area. Hunter carried a similar impression. Indeed, Hunter pointed out how the government had for long erred in assuming the Hindu caste system to be the only type of social organization in existence and thus misunderstood the composition of village society. He emphasized that the 'ethnic shape and structure of Bengal would remain largely unintelligible if the tribal component of the local population and the role of the tribal culture in shaping the local culture as a whole are ignored'.[11]

The increasing official awareness of the growing Hindu influence on the adivasi world was reflected in the methodology followed by Dalton in *Descriptive Ethnology* (1872).[12] While writing about 'Hinduized' and 'broken' tribes, Dalton presumably had in mind a much earlier phase of Hinduization. Yet it should be noted that he attempted a classification of some Bengal tribes on the basis of two principles: language and the extent of Hindu influence on the tribes. His classification of tribes as 'aborigines' and 'Hinduized aborigines' was obviously based on the principle of the extent of Hindu influence.

The elaborate official narrative of the radical Santal movement, the Kherwar movement (1874–82), provides for the first time the most explicit statement of the 'Hinduization' thesis. Some of these reports will be presented here in a chronological order, therfore repetitions are inevitable.

The Bhagalpur Commissioner, 7 October 1874.[13] He wrote of a mammoth Santal gathering, under the leadership of Bhagirath, at a place called Bowsee,

> the site of a Hindu temple in South Bhagalpur. . . . This was followed by the establishment at Tardiha, under Bhagirath's auspices, of a shrine conducted under Hindu principles, with a Santal *Pandah* [person in charge of the religious ceremonies]. A part of the system was that all professing followers of the new regime were required to kill their fowls and pigs with a view to purification. The movement took on enormously.

John Boxwell, Deputy Commissioner of the Santal Parganas, 1 October 1874.[14] The killing of 'impure' fowls and pigs continued over a vast area, almost as a 'religious act'. The numbers at the Santal assembly at the Tardiha shrine continued to swell. Here Bhagirath

> went through a number of ceremonies . . . and was marked on the forehead by a Hindoo, Matadin . . . with a red mark. . . . I have no doubt this man's [Matadin's] influence has given the colour of Hindooism to Bhagruth's movement. . . . I believe Bhagrut wished to become and did become the

leader of a great religious movement among the Sonthals. I believe that this pilgrimage [to the shrine] and purification is evidence of a strong tendency among the non-Aryan Sonthals to amalgamate with the Hindoos who surround them.

The Bhagalpur Commissioner's Annual General Report, 1874–5.[15] The report says a lot about the new 'purification' movement, evidently under the influence of Hinduism:

One very peculiar feature about the movement was the establishment of a small shrine for Mahadeb [a Hindu god] at Tardiha. . . . The Sonthals are at all times an easily excited race, and it is said by their officers [presumably leaders] that they are at this moment ripe for the acceptance of semi-Hindu ideas . . . the new system spread like a wild fire, and after slaughtering their animals, every one was in motion going to Tardiha to visit the shrine . . . those who favoured the new movement seemed to have started a distinguishing mark of their own, in the shape of what was called a 'bela-thika' (a mark with the paste made out of juice from *bel* leaves).

This points to Vaishnava influence. *The Bhagalpur Commissioner*, 25 February 1875.[16] Here, he emphatically wrote about 'the stronghold which Hinduism is taking of the Sonthal mind at the present moment'. He argued in favour of giving 'freedom to the movement', ceasing 'opposition to the wishes of the people if they desire . . . to assemble (in moderate numbers) for the purpose of exercising their religious feelings, but . . . we must by severe measures purge the movement of all the political connection of a doubtful kind which it now exhibits'.

The Bhagalpur Commissioner, 9 March 1875.[17] While suspecting that Bhagirath 'proceeded to turn his power to account by promoting a religious movement in the direction of Hinduism', the Commissioner was baffled by the extraordinary rapidity of the spread of the movement, and by the intense moral fervour of the Santals in doing whatever he had asked them to do, including killing of all impure birds and beasts, despite the fact that 'they formed a considerable item of property in every household'. All this, the Commissioner believed, amounted to a 'change of religion'.

Richard Temple, Lieutenant Governor of Bengal, 9 March 1875.[18] 'A sort of religious movement has been for some time past perceptible among them [Santals], and is fast increasing. They are leaving their aboriginal religion (if such it can be called) and joining Hindooism.'

The Deputy Commissioner of Santal Parganas, 16 March 1881.[19] The report, written in the context of the revival of the Kherwar movement in the climate of the widespread resistance to the census enumeration of the time, noted the growing strength of the 'movement' towards Hinduism. In very many villages 'the people slaughtered their pigs and poultry, either to signalize their having become pure or Hindus, or as preparatory to becoming so'. The leader was a Vaishnava guru, Dubia Gossain. When pressed by the census enumerators for stating their religion, the Santals, particularly 'the old kherwars', objected to being called Santals, and wanted instead to be called 'Hindus'.

W.M. Smith, Subdivisional Officer at Dumka (1881) also heard the rebel Santals denying their Santal ancestry. They resented being called Santal or Manjjhi, and preferred calling themselves 'Kherwar' of 'Ram Hindu Kherwar'. S.S. Jones, Assistant Commissioner of Rajmahal (1881), explicitly stated the dominant aim of the Kherwar movement: 'to mix in the social and religious scale by admission into Hinduism'. Rattray, Deputy Magistrate and Collector of Dumka (1881), was similarly convinced that the Kherwars 'follow the footsteps of the Hindu religion'. Writing on the regular visits of the Kherwars to the large fair at Bowsi, the site of a famous Hindu temple, to meet their new preceptors (gurus), such as Mangal Das, Thakur Gossain and Chandra Sadhu, all Vaishnavas, Captain Carnac, Assistant Commissioner, Santal Parganas (1881), asserted that their major purpose was 'simply to declare their affinity with Hinduism'.

One of the central themes of most official reports on the progress of the Kherwar movement was the 'abandonment' by the Santals of their old religion and their increasing assimilation into Hinduism, under the close guidance of Hindu preceptors, usually Vaishnavas. The officials believed that it was not just a fleeting fancy and they were aware of a split in Santal society between the traditionalists and the innovators over the religious issue.

The phenomenon of 'Hinduization', the bureaucrats of the colonial administration presumed, was not necessarily restricted to the tribal tracts plagued by widespread agrarian unrest. According to them, it was a general occurrence in the tribal world. Alfred Lyall characterized the growing Hindu influence as the 'gradual Brahmanising of the aboriginal, non-Aryan of casteless tribes'.[20] In 1884, the Bengal government wrote to the Government of India describing the phenomenon: 'The late census [1881] showed how rapidly the old aboriginal faiths are being effaced and what progress is being made in the absorption of the primitive race in the great system of Hinduism.'[21] In 1891, Risley highlighted for the first time the complexities and regional variations of the phenomenon of Hinduization. He indentified 'at least four distinct processes' which will be discussed later. He noted several instances where Hinduization had caused a complete effacement of the old tribal identity, and predicted that as a result of the process at work as he found it 'the tribe will soon have become a caste in the full sense of the word and will go on stripping itself of all customs likely to betray its true descent'. His assertion in 1915 was more pointed: 'All over India at the present moment tribes are gradually and insensibly being transformed into castes.'

The official representation of the alleged 'Hinduization' process, whether connected with large-scale tribal protest movements or not, is only partially valid. Regarding the Hinduization process, occurring outside the context of organized resistance, the official reports themselves contain conclusive evidence that it generally affected a tiny segment of tribal society, i.e. the relatively well-off group. The process was far more complex where it was immediately linked with the radical agrarian movement. In this use, the adoption of Hindu cultural traits was a collective effort. Indeed, the emulation was part of the conscious strategy of the rebels to be better equipped to cope with their powerful adversaries. The conscious emulation was also clearly selective. Only some particular Hindu traits, relating more to religious beliefs and ethical norms than to the specific Hindu caste-based social organization, were borrowed. More importantly, the rebel tribals were simultaneously keen on this emulation and on preserving their identity. This scarcely meant their assimilation into the 'Hindufold'.

Observations on the extract cited earlier from the 1833 report on the Bhumij revolt clearly shed light on the limitations of the Hinduization process there, a fact evident from the survival of some crucial elements of the tribal religious faith. The researches of Dalton[22] and Risley[23] confirm the findings of the 1833 report. A striking observation in Risley's writings on the Bhumij is the unevenness of the spread of Hindu influence in the Bhumij tract.

Dalton, too, like the 1833 report assumed a ' common origin' of the Bhumij and the Munda (sometimes referred to as Kols by him):

> Near the boundary of Chutia Nagpur . . . the Kols who form the bulk of the population call themselves Mundas. . . . The title Bhumij . . . is given to the members of the tribe settled further east. . . . Those who live in the proximity of Chutia Nagpur recognise no distinction between themselves and the Mundas. They intermarry and associate with and coalesce in all matters indicating identity of race. . . . The Bhumij further east have become too Hinduized to acknowledge the relationship. The Dhalbhum Bhumij consider themselves autochthones, and will not admit that they are in any way connected with the Mundas, Hos, or Santals. It is pretty certain that the zamindars of all these estates are of the same race as their people.

Dalton also noted, like the 1833 report, that the Dhalbhum Bhumij 'observes many of the Hindu festivals but retain their sacred groves in which they still sacrifice to the old gods'.

Risley had something new to add, particularly with regard to the differential diffusion of Hindu influence in well-marked regions of the Bhumij country and among different sections of Bhumij society. Like Dalton, he believed 'that the Bhumij are nothing more than a branch of the Mundas, who have spread to the eastward, mingled with the Hindus, and thus for the most part severed their connection with the parent tribe'.[24] The Hindu influence noticeably increased as the Bhumij migrated eastward. For instance, the Bhumij of western Manbhum, inhabiting the tract of the country lying on both sides of the river Subarnarekha and bounded on the east by the Ajodhya Hill range, 'are beyond doubt pure Mundas. . . . This region contains an enormous number of Mundari graveyards, and may fairly be considered as one of the earliest settlements of the Munda race.' However, 'on the eastern side of the Ajodhya range, which forms a complete barrier to ordinary communication, all is changed. Both the Mundari language and the title of Munda have dropped out of use, and the aborigines of this eastern tract called themselves Bhumij or Sardar, and talk Bengali.'[25] The Hindu influence was differentially diffused socially as well:

> The religion of the Bhumij varies, within certain limits, according to the social position and territorial status of the individuals concerned. Zamindars and well-to-do tenure-holders employ Brahmins as their family priests and offer sacrifices to Kali or Mahamaya [Hindu goddess]. The mass of the people revere the sun under the names of Sing-bonga and Dharm, as the giver of harvests to men and the cause of all changes of seasons affecting their agricultural fortunes. They also worship a host of minor gods. . . . The upper classes employ Brahmins of their own, and ignore the cult of the earlier gods; while the mass of the tribe are guided in the regular observances by the teachings of the *layas* or priests of the forest gods, and only call in the assistance of Brahmins on the comparatively rare occasions when it is deemed necessary to propitiate one of the standard Hindu deities. But the Brahmins who serve the Bhumij zamindar or tenure-holder as a family priest takes a higher place in the local community of Brahmins than the casual Brahmin who ministers to the spiritual needs of the ordinary cultivator. The former will call himself a Rahri Kulin, and will be received on equal terms by all members of the sacred order, while the latter belongs to a much lower class, and associates with the comparatively degraded Brahmins who work for *Kurmis* [an agricultural caste] and *Dhobas* [washermen].[26]

The four typical processes[27] of 'Hinduization' identified by Risley revealed the limitations of the phenomenon of Hinduization and also partly the differential diffusion of Hindu influence. The first stands somewhat apart, illustrating the decisiveness of the role of a few affluent groups, evidently largely separated form the tribal collectivity. Here the initiative lay with 'independent landed proprietors', keen on upholding their pretensions to non-tribal descent:

They usually set up as Rajputs; their first step being to start a Brahmin priest, who invents for them a mythical ancestor, supplies them with a family miracle connected with the locality where their tribe are settled, and discovers that they belong to some hitherto unheard-of clan of the great Rajput community. An important step towards consolidation of the new status was the establishment of matrimonial alliances outside the traditional endogamous group, . . . they intermarry, if not with pure Rajputs, at least with a superior order of manufactured Rajputs, whose promotion into the Brahmanical system dates far enough back for the steps by which it was gained to have become forgotten. Thus a real change of blood may take place; while in any case the tribal name is completely lost, and with it all possibility of accurately separating this class of people form the Hindus of pure blood, and of assigning them to any non-Aryan tribe. They have been absorbed in the fullest sense of the word, and henceforth pose, and are locally accepted, as high caste Hindus. All stages of the process, family miracle and all, can be illustated by actual instances taken from the leading families of Chotanagpur.

Risley's description of the second process does not point to any role of such ambitious families in Hinduization. It occurred where 'a number of aborigines embrace the tenets of a Hindu religious sect, losing thereby their tribal name and becoming Vaisnabas, Ramayats and the like'. There may or may not have been an admixture of blood. 'Anyway the identity of the converts as aborigines is usually, though not invariably, lost, and this also may therefore be regarded as a case of true absorption.' The third process involved presumably a larger segment of the tribe: 'A whole tribe of aborigines, or a large section of the tribes enrol themselves in the ranks of Hinduism under the style of a new caste, which, though claiming an origin of remote antiquity, is readily distinguishable by its name from any standard and recognised castes.' This was how

the great majority of the Koch inhabitants of Rungpore now invariably describe themselves as Rajbansis or Bhanga Kshatriyas—a designation which enabled them to represent themselves as an outlying branch of the Kshatriyas who fled to north-eastern Bengal in order to escape from the wrath of Parasuram [a mythical hero vowing extirpation of Kshatriyas] . . . they keep Brahmans, imitate the Brahmanical ritual in their marriage ceremony, and have begun to adopt the Brahmanical system of gotras.

Risley's illustration of the fourth process has been discussed earlier, the phenomenon of 'conversion to Hinduism' among 'the Bhumij of western Bengal'. He found the process distinctive in that 'A whole tribe of aborigines, a section of the tribe, become gradually converted to Hinduism without, like the Rajbansis, abandoning their tribal designation.'

Of these four processes, the first and the last were limited to a handful of powerful, affluent landholders. Emulation of Hindu culture was for them a conscious means of consolidating their position and status and distancing themselves from the tribal milieu to which they had once belonged. The last process occurring in the Bhumij tract was identical. Risley explicitly made two points. First, the Hindu influence was differentially diffused socially. 'The religion of the Bhumij varies, within certain limits, according to the social position and territorial status [landed status] of the individuals concerned.' Second, the social status of the Brahmins officiating for this elite group was far superior to that of the Brahmin who 'ministers to the spiritual needs of the ordinary cultivator'. This explicit statement about the limitations of the Hinduization process contradicts his following general assertion:

> Here a pure Dravidian race have lost their original language and now speak only Bengali; they worship Hindu gods in addition to their own (the tendency being to relegate the tribal gods to the women) and the more advanced among them employ Brahmans as family priests. They still retain a set of totemistic exogamous subdivisions closely resembling those of the Mundas and the Santals. But they are beginning to forget the totems which the names of subdivisions denote, and the names themselves will probably soon be abandoned in favour of more aristocratic designation. The tribe will then have become a caste in the full sense of the word and will go on stripping itself of all customs likely to betray its true descent.[28]

The second process, restricted to small communities, did not perhaps occur among any of the chosen tribes. The Rajbansis, the alleged Hinduization of whom illustrates the third process, also lie outside the scope of this study. Nevertheless, their case will be discussed here because of the applicability to it of observations made on the first and the last process occurring in some parts of the tribal belt of south Bihar. Here, too, the Hindu influence was differentially diffused socially. The initiative in the emulation of Hindu influence invariably wholly came from the elite Rajbansi groups. The motivation, too, ensured for them a secure place in the Hindu caste hierarchy, an aim difficult to achieve because of the consistent opposition to their efforts from the high caste Hindus. The idioms they used while contesting the pretensions of caste Hindus did attract even the common Rajbansis. They were, however, reluctant to admit the latter into the preserve of their newly acquired status. In fact, the sharp inequality in respect of the material position of the two groups tended to reinforce the cultural barriers that the elite Rajbansis created between themselves and their poor brethren.

The Rajbansi movement, in the typical form in which it developed in the late nineteenth century, was essentially an organized assertion by a section of the Koch of a claim of a superior ritual status in the Hindu caste hierarchy. During the 1881 census operations, the Koch denied their traditional tribal name and insisted on being called Hindu Kshatriyas, a status they claimed to have once possessed a long time ago. The immediate occasion for the assertion of the Koch claim was the organized opposition to it from high caste Hindus. Indeed, the strength of the opposition persuaded the census authority to reject the claim. The intense resentment and bitterness that this caste Hindu 'intrigue' created among the Koch not only strengthened the Rajbansi movement, but also created conditions for the broad-based solidarity movement directed against the caste Hindus. The confidence and the moral fervour characterizing the movement throughout was largely derived from the leadership provided by a resourceful Koch group, which resented the 'arrogance' of the caste Hindus all the more because of its affluence and the resultant sense of power. The usual idioms of the counter-ideology developed for contesting the caste Hindu assertions also attracted the rank and file of the Koch community and considerably strengthened the social base of the movement. However, the perceptible Hindu influence was largely restricted to the Rajbansi elites, the economically and socially powerful group in this society. The social movement insisting on the appropriation of the status symbols and rituals of high caste Hindus only marginally influenced the far larger segment of the Rajbansi community consisting of the poor, the landless and also the numerous groups of destitute share-croppers. The 'reforms' on which the Rajbansi leadership laid so much of stress, such as prohibition of women's labour in agriculture, the practice of widow remarriage, and alcoholic drinks and pork eating, all conflicted with the cultural traditions of Rajbansi society. Forbidding women's labour in agriculture and various non-domestic works would substantially reduce the income of most Koch families. Furthermore, the leadership did not at all want all Koch families, regardless of their economic and social position, admitted to the ritual status it itself had aspired to. It was particularly averse to the idea of allowing all families to wear the sacred thread, which, it was believed, would remove the stigma of belonging to low castes. The expense incurred in the sacred thread ceremony inevitably restricted the innovation to a few wealthy families. Even where some others could afford the cost, the leadership resisted the idea of throwing open the practice. In fact, the leadership's obduracy in the matter split Rajbansi society into several rival factions.

None of Risley's four test cases proves his assertion about the so-called tribe-caste continuum. The origins, implications and ramifications of the alleged 'Hinduization' process among the Santal, the Munda, the Oraon and the Ho, as observed from official records, are far more complex in nature. The process as it occurred illustrates the argument presented earlier that the growth of Hindu influence in this vast tribal world did not lead to its articulation with the caste-based and hierarchical Hindu social organization, or even with the specific economic organization of the Hindu neighbourhood. 'Hindu influence' and 'detribalization' were far from identical phenomena. Indeed, emulation of Hindu cultural traits was essentially a conscious means of the tribal identity and solidarity in the context of an intensifying resistance to the enemy.

First the Santal case will be discussed. Till the beginning of the Kherwar movement (1874) the local administration was presumably unaware of Hindu influence on Santal society. However, there is evidence of this influence even during the first Santal revolt (1855). It is not known if systematic and organized efforts of the kind characterizing the Kherwar movement were now made towards a conscious emulation of some particular aspects of Hindu faith and culture. A few instances of the Hindu influence, particularly on the Santal leaders, Sidhu and Kanu, will be examined here. *Thakur* (derived from a Sanskrit synonym for God or one of His images) was the name by which they addressed the God that 'appeared' before them on a full-moon day in April 1855, commanding them to lead the revolt against the alien exploiters of the Santal race. The supreme creator in the Santal cosmogony was called 'Marang Baru'. The appearance of God before an individual was not consistent either with the Santal religious beliefs. The place where the leaders asked their followers to come to worship the incarnated God was not the traditional 'sacred grove' of the Santal village, but an improvised structure, though not resembling a Hindu temple. The Santal village priest or headman, normally presiding over the Santal religious ceremonies, had no role whatsoever in this worship. The elaborate rituals of the worship, particularly the strict injunctions of the leaders to the followers to perform the rituals with the utmost 'purity of mind' also point to Hindu influence. The leaders were also familiar with the Hindu concept of *yugas* (epochs), i.e. *Satya, Treta, Dwapar* and *Kali*, and with the concept of the phenomenal changes marking the passage from one epoch to another. However, as mentioned earlier, whether any organized intiative was taken for 'reforming' Santal society, its religious and ethical practices on the model of the borrowed Hindu ideas, is not known.

It was the rapid growth of the radical Kherwar movement that made the colonial administration realize for the first time the considerable extent of Hindu influence on the Santals. The discussion here will be based largely on the contemporary official reports[29] on the progress and organization of the movement, and not on a later account of it by O'Malley in *District Gazetteer Santal Parganas* (1910).[30] The point to be discussed is whether the official characterization of the movement as a clear evidence of Santal society's 'amalgamation' with the Hindu religious and social system is valid or not.

The movement of 1874, led by Bhagirath Manjhi of the Godda subdivision of Santal Parganas, whom the Santals regarded as their messiah, as they did Sidhu and Kanu, leaders of the insurrection of 1885, 'spread like wild fire'. Two of his associates carried on the movement after his arrest. Prompt police action checked its growth. However, its distinct organization survived, as indicated by a police report which stated that it 'has been silently spreading and strengthening'.

Hindu influence on the movement is evident from the religious ideas, rituals and practices associated with it, and also from the social origins of the preceptors (gurus) inspiring it. It had the usual attributes of what anthropologists have called 'religious revitalization' movement, its central focus being the 'revitalization' of the existing religious and ethical life as the basis of the 'reconstruction' of the social order. The 'revitalization', only marginally stressed in the 1855 movement, now constituted its crucial concern. The doctrinal basis of the revitalization programme was largely provided by Hinduism. It was at a Hindu shrine in the Godda subdivision that Bhagirath first (July 1874) announced his divine status, proclaimed his consecration as the 'King' of the Santal Raj and disclosed to his followers his general plans for their 'purification'. He was marked on his forehead by a devout Hindu, Matadin, an 'ex-Mutineer', whom he had first met at the Bhagalpur jail. A new shrine, dedicated to the Hindu god Mahadev, was built soon after. The revitalization movement initially stressed the idea of the substitution of one God for the many local *bongas* (spirits) worshipped by the Santals, and the idea of a cleaner (*sapha*) life. One of the major themes of the 'thousands of anonymous letters found to be circulating through the villages' towards the end of 1880 was that 'to avoid calamity the Santals were to take the name of God daily'. Becoming a *Sapha Hor* (clean man) necessitated several things: abandonment of the practice of rearing pigs and fowl; killing of the entire breed of such 'unclean' beasts and birds; giving up the 'ancient custom of eating beefs, ham, pork and others'; replacement of 'their time-honoured habits of drunkenness and debauchery by a stricter course of life'; clean personal habits including a daily bath and wearing of clean clothes; and complete dissociation from the practices of witchcraft. The idea of abstention from work on Sundays was probably the result of Christian influence, though in general the *Sapha Hors* resented the Christians. The wearing of a mark on the forehead was a distinctively Vaishnava ritual.[31] Quite a few of the *Sapha Hors* also wore the sacred thread like the Brahmins. However, the Kherwar leaders did not ever assert that this was an essential part of the new creed.

Insistence by the leaders on such an elaborate 'moral code' for the followers thus meant a sharp break with the traditional Santal lifestyle and culture. True that monotheistic belief, which had a crucial role in the religious revitalization movement, was not entirely alien to the Santal religious tradition. This, at least, was the belief of the Santal gurus, whom the Santals deeply venerated as interpreters of their oral traditions.[32] However, the old belief in one supreme God now scarcely influenced the day-to-day Santal religious practices.

It is notable that the Kherwars were made aware of Hindu ideas by the itinerant Vaishnava preachers locally known as *Babajis* or *Gossains*. Some of their teachings which must have attracted the Santals were their rejection of the hierarchical Hindu caste organization and the emphasis on love, equality and brotherhood as the basis of human relationships. Such teachings had much to do with the social composition of these itinerant Vaishnavas, who formed a dissident Hindu sect. An official report described them as 'miserable low caste Hindus who from time to time travel through their [Santal] neighbourhood'. Dubia, an influential leader of the later phase of the Kherwar movement (1881–2) was called Gosain.

The selective borrowing of Hindu cultural traits as the basis of the Kherwar revitalization movement has erroneously been referred is as 'Hinduization' largely because the motivations of the Kherwars in this regard and the particular historical context in which this emulation had taken place have not been properly understood. Influential Hindus in the locality and some government officials offered almost similar explanations of the motivations. Taresh Nath Nandy, Pakour zamindar, believed that the 'Santals, struck with the disparity between their own status and that of the Hindus around them, who were showing signs of life and improvement in every direction, were fired with a desire of bettering their own social and religious condition as preliminary to gaining political rights.' Captain Carmac, Assistant Commissioner of the Santal Parganas, similarly expressed,

> The object of the Kherwar movement was originally solely social religion. The Santals craved for a better state; their inferiority to their neighbours must have been felt amongst them. And they set up something more advanced and purer religion and higher social code, something to bring them on a par with their neighbours. The term 'Banga Santal', 'Boka Santal' [stupid Santal], so frequently used towards them by their Hindu neighbours must have been very galling.[33]

This line of reasoning partly anticipates the notion of 'rank concession syndrome' propounded by Martin Orans,[34] a professional anthropologist, while explaining the considerable increase in the scale of the Santal emulation of some Hindu religious rituals and practices after the abortive insurrection of 1855. The views of some professional anthropologists on the alleged Hinduization of tribes will be examined later. However, this specific view of Orans will be discussed here.

Orans' view may be summed up as follows. It was not just coincidental that the more systematic borrowing of some Hindu religious rituals and practices followed the failure of the 1855 revolt in achieving its aim—the political aim of overthrowing the alien (*dikku*) domination and the social aim of elevating the 'rank' of the Santal community. The adoption of Hindu practices was a result of the realization by Santals that repeating the kind of anti-*dikku* struggle organized in 1855 would be a fruitless and, indeed, expensive venture. Their major emphasis thereafter was on 'economic improvement through rank improvement'. They more systematically emulated the 'Hindu rank model' out of a conviction that it was superior to theirs. The 'rank concession syndrome' is precisely this explicit acceptance by the Santals of the superiority of the Hindu 'rank'. An instance of the symbols of Hindu 'rank' emulated by the Santals was the wearing of the sacred thread. 'A prime motivation for the [Kherwar] sect's adoption of such practices [as wearing of the sacred thread] must have been to attain higher rank.'

Two questions need to be answered here. Did the apparent failure of the 1855 revolt lead the Santals to forsake for ever the 'political path'? Would it be proper to characterize their aim in emulating Hindu traits merely as 'rank improvement'? The answer would also be relevant to the examination of the official view that the Santals had been rapidly becoming Hindus. It is true that the ruthless suppression of the revolt of 1855 and their consequent immiserization made the Santals wary of a violent political struggle. This, however, scarcely meant rejection altogether of political struggle in any form. They eschewed violence as far as possible, but consistently pursued a political goal, i.e. the creation of an independent Santal Raj. The reconstruction of their belief and ethical systems through the emulation of Hindu practices was regarded by them as an essential precondition for achieving their goal. The leaders emphasized all along that the coming of the 'Great Day' would be indefinitely put off till they 'purified' themselves. The emulation was only marginally designed to promote 'economic improvement through rank improvement'. It would be misleading to isolate it from the wider millenarian framework of the Santal's active political will. Orans' interpretation of the Santals' motivations in borrowing Hindu norms is thus of doubtful validity. He was mistaken in delinking the so-called 'rank improvement' from the wider political vision of the Santals. In fact, 'rank improvement' was only part of a broader political strategy. Contemporary official reports on the rise and progress of the Kherwar movement (1874–82) highlight its distinct political character. Its political overtones were pronounced from the very beginning. At the Bowsee meeting referred to earlier, as Boxwell, Deputy Commissioner of Santal Parganas, came to know, 'great numbers of men, counted singly, talked about the old *Hul* [insurrection of 1855], about old *Sabahs* [divinely inspired leaders of the 1885 revolt]. Thakur [God] and a raj [independent Santal state].'[35] According to a missionary, Bhagirath, the leader, was their 'appointed King', and 'prayers made for the success of the new Santal raj'. The missionary also noted the sudden change that had occurred in the Santal outlook after their return from Bowsee. It was then that 'his followers began giving themselves airs and talking largely of the good times that were coming; that their day had come; that the shahibs would either be killed or driven out of the country, and that they would send the native Christians to the other world'. After Bhagirath's arrest Gyan Manjhi, one of his followers, planned what the Bhagalpur Commissioner called an 'audacious thing'. He issued *parwanahs* (authoritative orders) saying that he had the authority of the *Burra Sahib*, i.e. the Commissioner, for informing the people that they should not pay rent pending a new settlement. Following Gyan's arrest, the Santals of Rajmahal began to assemble at a place called Burtolla and proclaimed the country their own.[36] By 1880–1 the Santals were much less cautious in publicly proclaiming their political plans and the local officers could more confidently write about their real feelings. According to a missionary, the Kherwar Santals informed the other villagers not belonging to the sect: 'The land is ours. We cleared the jungles. We ought not to pay rent. We will combine and drive out the English.' They confidently asserted: 'The shahibs and Christians are few. We *Safas* [clean Santals] are numerous; the country will be ours; it will be our raj.'[37] The Santals, the Bhagalpur Commissioner felt, were comparable to the Irish peasants who 'have a dream about days which are to come to their race, when no rents will have to be paid, and, to touch this chord, will any time secure access to an intriguer or adventurer'. He thus concluded:

> We must recognise more than we have done of the features of the Santal character, that whatever may be his outward manners for the moment, he is by constitution politically discontented and aiming at a change. Moreover, a system has been formulated under the term Kherwar which by mixing up national ideas along with matters connected with social and religious reforms, presents a view thoroughly attractive to the Santal mind, and has created an organization necessarily opposed to government.[38]

The political orientation of the movement was reflected in the elaborate organization gradually built up for sustaining the movement. The organization, much stronger than the one of 1855, depended on the pre-existing secret societies, formed in the 1840s, and also on the organization, where it survived, which the two leaders of the 1855 revolt, Sidhu and Kanu, created, after the 'divine incarnation', to pursue their radical goals. The greatest binding force in the Kherwar sect was, however, loyalty to the new 'religion'. A contemporary report described the elements of strength in the Kherwar organization:

> The Kherwars are a closely united community, and keep up inter-communication in matters religious, social and political in the most wonderful way. Many letters, or *parwanahs*, as they call them, were circulated, addressed from one brotherhood met together in one assembly, to another assembly, or to a particular person.

At the same time, the tradition of their earlier secret societies continued. As one missionary noted, 'their meetings were held at night, and they are very careful to keep their deliberations secret'. Given the pervasive political ferment in which the Kherwar movement took shape (the revival at the time of the ancient Santal tribal name 'Kherwar' being undoubtedly an expression of this radical Santal mood), the emulation by the Santals of a few Hindu rituals and practices scarcely led to their 'detribalization' or to their articulation with the hierarchical Hindu caste organization. The rituals and practices were mostly related to their 'purification' programme. They did not adopt the entire gamut of Hindu practices. The wearing of the sacred thread during the Kherwar movement was confined to a small group, and even here this did not signify the symbol of any ritual ranking of this negligible minority. The Kherwar movement was in this respect distinguishable from the Rajbansi movement. The Rajbansi leadership, as has been noted earlier, wanted to restrict the 'privilege' of wearing the sacred thread to a small affluent and powerful group. In this case the privilege symbolized a newly acquired ritual status.

Despite the gradual weakening of the organized Kherwar

movement after 1882, the Kherwar ideology continued to hold sway. The periodic 'outbursts of Kherwarism' whenever any serious 'calamity' struck the Santal country were mostly sporadic, localized events basically different from the recent protest movements of the Kherwars. Relapses into the old life-style also inevitably occurred, particularly where scrupulous observance of the Kherwar norms, such as prohibition of rearing of 'unclean' beasts and birds, greatly reduced the income of the converts' households.

Yet, Kherwar ideals continued to exert a vital influence on Santal society, or at least a segment of it. Though the Kherwar organization ceased to be centrally controlled, and was split into three groups—Safai, Babaji and Samra[39]—there was not much of a difference in their ideals. However, there was one striking change: the Kherwar rituals were combined in some cases with elements of the Santal tradition. Of the three Kherwar sects, Samra was perhaps the most rigid in the observance of the norms of 'purification'. Admission to the sect was strictly controlled. Santals keen on joining it had to take solemn oaths before the guru as well as the community, binding them to follow punctiliously its prescribed ideas and practices, particularly an oath to give up completely *bonga* (spirit) worship. The Kherwar guru had seldom insisted on such oaths earlier. A measure of the continuing influence of the Kherwar ideology was the widespread practice of the sect gurus presiding over the crucial 'rites of passage' in the Santal village, i.e. ceremonies connected with birth, attainment of adulthood, marriage and death. The village priest or headman had earlier been the sole actor in all these rituals. On the other hand, elements of the Santal tradition were now traceable in the recent practices of the sect members. For instance, powers of healing diseases were attributed to the *babajis*, earlier perceived primarily as guides with respect to the 'purification' programme. In the Santal perception, the *babajis* were indistinguishable from the traditional Santal *Ojhas* curing diseases through their alleged supernatural powers. The Santals themselves assured the role of Kherwar gurus, while previously all of them were Hindu Vaishnavas.

It is, however, difficult to estimate the size of the Santal population actively practising the Kherwar ideals. It seems the number, perhaps never significant, tended to decline when the organized Kherwar movement gradually petered out. The extent of Hindu influence later on the Santal world has sometimes been misjudged by officials. In fact, some bureaucrats of the colonial administration had attempted to correct an erroneous impression in this regard. The census data (1921 and 1931) showing a considerable increase in the number of 'Hindu' Santals during the decade 1921–31 was generally interpreted as evidence that the Santals had been forsaking their traditional religion. Hutton, Census Commissioner of India (1931), questioned the authenticity of the data recorded by the local enumerators, attributing part of the increase in the number of 'Hindu' Santals to the systematic propaganda by some Hindu organizations working among the Santals to mention their religion as 'Hinduism'. 'The census figures of 1931,' he concluded, 'were to some extent vitiated by a communalist campaign to return all tribal religions as Hindu.' However, he did admit an increase in Hindu influence, 'even allowing for this there has been a great decrease in tribal religions (a decrease of 15.3 per cent since 1921) in spite of a great increase in the tribal population. This decrease is almosty entirely due to defections from these religions to Christianity and to Hinduism.'[40] However, William Archer (Census Superintendent of Bihar, 1939–41 and Deputy Commissioner of the Santal Parganas, 1945–6) differently interpreted the census data.

> Aboriginals as a whole have no terms of their own to describe their religion. . . . When a tribesman says his religion is Hindu, he often merely means that he is not a Christian or Mohammadan. He certainly never implies that he has shed all his tribal ways, that he has adopted Brahmanic practices. . . . Even if he adopts certain Hindu festivals, it is often because they afford him fresh excuses for jollity. . . . Moreover, Hinduism . . . has always been tolerant of variety and there is nothing in Hindu theory or practice to prevent a tribesman from retaining all his tribal practices and yet being accepted as a Hindu.[41]

The nature of the Hindu influence on the Munda movement (1895–1900), the Tana Bhagat movement of the Oraons (1914–22) and the Ho movement (in the 1930s) also illustrate the argument that Hindu influence and 'Hinduization'(and the resultant 'detribalization') were not identical phenomena.

As elsewhere, Hindu influence gradually spread in the Munda world, but its extent was not perhaps significant till the Birsa movement (1894–1900). Initially, the influence was largely restricted to the Munda Raj family, the Nagbansi family. It called itself Hindu, increasingly Hinduized the state rituals, lavishly patronized the Brahmins it had persuaded to settle there through rent-free lands and appointed a considerable number of Hindus in the different branches of administration. However, it had not taken the initiative whatsoever in popularizing the Hindu faith in the Munda villages. The two main agencies which played a role in the spread of Hindu ideas were the itinerant Vaishnava gurus, and the migrant artisan communities, such as blacksmiths, potters and weavers, whose services the local village economy urgently needed. The Vaishnava preachers seldom stayed in the village for more than a few days. The Mundas, therefore, imbibed the rudiments of the Hindu faith mostly from the artisans. Whatever its historical basis, there is a view arguing that it was from them and other Hindus that the Mundas (and other adivasis) learnt the charms or spells (*mantras*) effective against the deadly menace of witchcraft.

That the Hindu influence became considerable in the Munda villages in the late nineteenth century is evident from the Munda leader Birsa's close contacts with a few Hindu learned men and preachers. K.S. Singh, the eminent historian of the Birsa movement, has traced the Hindu influence on Birsa to his contacts with Anand Pande, a devout Hindu, and another 'Vaisnava monk'.[42] Pande, whom Birsa met 'probably in 1890', 'was well-versed in the rudimentary form of Vaisnavism that prevailed in the area and with the Hindu epic-lores, and enjoyed some local reputation and influence. . . . He [Birsa] stayed with him for three years.' Birsa's contact with the 'Vaisnava monk' was shorter—just two months and a half. 'Under his influence he [Birsa] did not give up eating meat altogether. He adopted the sacred thread, worshipped the *tulsi* plant [its leaves being considered sacred by Hindus], wore the Sandal mark, familiarized himself with Hindu concept of epochs and prohibited cow-slaughter.' His disciples also claimed that Birsa 'had the vision of Mahaprabhu Vishnu Bhagwan [a Hindu god], which marked the consummation of the Vaisnav influence on their master'.

However, Hindu influence on the Munda movement in general and presumably on Birsa, too, can be traced earlier than 1890. The way it spread is significant. As in the Santal world, so here too, the spread is not intelligible outside the context of the growing agrarian unrest in the Munda villages. The Mundas became aware of the basic elements of the religious revitalization movement before the emergence of Birsa's charismatic leadership. The Birsa movement would not otherwise have spread as rapidly as it did.

Official reports indicate that Hindu influence had become marked as early as 1881–2, the time of the second Kherwar movement. The Mundas became aware of the movement partly because parts of Chotanagpur were contiguous to the Santal Parganas, and in Chotanagpur itself there were large pockets of Santal settlements. The main channel of transmission of Hindu influence was the Munda contacts with Dubia Gosain, the 'spiritual' leader of the second Kherwar movement. The Mundas wanted him to advise them in all matters relating to the crucial 'land question'. As the Chotanagpur Commissioner's annual report of 1880–2 noted, Dubia

> was visited by some of the malcontents of Lohardugga, who had not been satisfied with the decisions of the Chotanagpur Tenures Act [Chotanagpur Landlord and Tenants Procedures Act, 1879], and he certainly encouraged them to hope that they might gain possession of the lands they claimed. . . . This led some few Kols [Mundas] to forbid rents being paid in one estate, saying that they were only due to Kol rulers.[43]

Dubia's advice was evidently not confined to the immediate agrarian grievances of the Mundas. The Commissioner described the sources of his influence in 'all the districts' of the Chotanagpur Division, attributing it partly to his alleged miracle-making powers:

> . . . the prophecies and miracles of now notorious *faquir* (*fakir*, a saint) Dubai Gossain caused considerable excitement among the peoples of Hazaribagh and Lohardugga. . . . He held out hopes of fighting land and

other grievances. A number of letters were circulated in his name, the authenticity of which, however, he subsequently denied, but these letters produced more effect in the Sonthal Parganas than they did in the immediate neighbourhood of his residence. People were enjoined not to keep fowls and pigs—an order which was largely carried out by the Sonthals. At the same time order went round prohibiting ploughing on Sundays and the use of cows and bullocks for ploughing. . . . Some letters bearing the name of the Gossain enjoined all Sonthals to bathe and shave, and to adopt other ceremonial observances of the Hindoos on the occasions of births and deaths. For some time the Gossain exerted great influence on the people, and alms and contributions flowed freely for his support.[44]

The basic similarity between the Kherwar revitalization movement and that which Birsa initiated, on a limited scale in 1895 and on a much larger scale in 1899–1990, points to the influence of Bhagirath and Dubai Gossain. Whatever the Christian influence on Birsa, it did not have much to do with the distinctive trends in the Munda revitalization movement.

In order to understand the precise nature of Hindu influence on the Birsa movement and the nature of the relationship between religion and politics of the Mundas three questions need to be answered: (1) Would it be a valid argument that by conviction Birsa was primarily a social and religious reformer and that his eventual choice of the political path was explicable by the presence in his movement of hard core leaders of the Sardar movement?[45] (2) Can it be concluded that Birsa's first movement (1894–5), unlike the second (1899–1900), was mostly oriented to social and religious reforms in Munda society? (3) Did Birsa's attitude to the traditional Munda culture perceptibly change during his second movement?

It is true that Birsa was at one time sceptical of the fruitfulness of the use of violence in achieving the Munda aims. This, he feared, could well be counter-productive, because of the colonial state's superior command of the means of violence, and the use of these means could severely dislocate Munda economy and society. The 'purification' of the Munda race, he believed, would create in them enough moral power to cope with the enemy. However, he did not specify how moral reassurance would enable the Mundas to eliminate the alien domination in different forms over the Munda villages. This only reveals Birsa's indecisiveness about the right methods of coping with the enemy. Even assuming that the Sardars did have a role in persuading Birsa to choose the 'political' path, their perceptions of political aims and methods basically differed from those of Birsa. The Sardars, claiming descent from the village founders' families, had a limited political aim: restoration of their lost rights over their ancestral villages. Their method was reliance on constitutional means, inevitably necessitating dependence on the machinery of the colonial state itself, because without its formal approval of the Sardars' status in the village lands, the gains from their struggle with the enemy would be largely inconclusive. In contrast, Birsa's political aim was a radical one: the establishment of the Munda Raj, which was premised on the elimination of the entire system of alien domination, the colonial state being one of the aliens. The crucial feature of his method—the moral and spiritual regeneration of the Munda race—scarcely figured in the Sardars' plans of action. The Sardar movement had in it nothing comparable to Birsa's political vision.

As regards the second question, it will be argued that Birsa, aware as he was of his essentially political goal, i.e. establishment of the Munda Raj, was initially uncertain about the means of achieving the goal. The phrasing of his perceptions in the initial phase of his movement may create an impression that the central focus of his plan of action was primarily moral and spiritual regeneration of the Munda race. However, for him, the revitalization movement and the anti-alien political movement were parts of an integral philosophy and plan of action. He was fairly familiar with the recent history of Munda resistance, and he himself had played a role in the movement against the forest laws restricting the traditional access of the Mundas to forest resources. His choice of the political path was, therefore, far from an abrupt decision, unconnected with his awareness of the Munda political aspirations. This was the reason why Birsa's social and political philosophy constantly transcended the limited confines of the revitalization movement.

His very first pronouncement after the launch of his first movement (August 1895) brings out the essentially political orientation of his activity. He called himself a 'prophet' sent by God to announce the imminent end of this 'sinful' world,[46] after a mighty deluge. Of the 'sins' which the deluge would wash away he had a clear notion: the government, the money-based exchange economy of the time, and curiously, agriculture. His assertion that the deluge 'would sweep away government' points to his conviction that the establishment of the Munda Raj was premised on the destruction of the apparatus of power of the colonial state. He realized how the spread of the money-based economy facilitated alien control and domination over the Munda villages. His rejection of this economy led him to announce that 'all rupees in the world would become water and everyone should therefore spend what they have and buy cloths'. He did not quite explain, as the leaders of the Oraon Tana Bhagat movement later did, why he regarded agriculture as a sin. What, asked the leaders, had the Oraons gained from agriculture for which they had tried so hard for years? The aliens had misappropriated the largest part of the products of their labour—the crops and even the lands. It would not, therefore, be worthwhile for the Oraons to continue to cultivate their lands. The leaders, however, did not specify what the alternative means of livelihood should be. Nor did Birsa, who perhaps thought alike. How would the deluge come about? What precisely would his followers do to make it happen? If it happened how would his followers survive it ? With regard to all these questions, Birsa's thinking had a religious tinge. As in most millennial movements all over the world, Birsa believed that human efforts had no direct role in bringing about the deluge. Only a divine agency could do it. People of the earth would just eagerly await the cataclysmic happening with the purest of minds and hearts. He repeatedly told his followers to lead 'good lives' and to abstain from 'doing *puja* to *bhuts*', i.e. worship of spirits. He had a message of reassurance only for the followers of his precepts. Only they would survive, and 'the only safe place would be a plot of rising ground on which he had fixed his abode'.

The obscure elements in his religious thinking gradually

disappeared and his emphasis shifted to more precise ethical notions, religious beliefs and practices. He introduced a new set of austere, moral code, cleaner religious practices and rituals. Realizing that the assimilation of his new ideas by the Mundas necessitated sustained indoctrination, he carefully selected a group of preachers (*pracharakas*) entrusting to them the task of preaching his doctrines.[47] In fact, the difference between his two movements did not lie in the relative importance of the religious reforms and the 'political path'. The continuity between the two is unmistakable. There were two notable differences. First, Birsa's earlier indecisiveness about the 'political path' now disappeared. Second, an elaborate organization coordinating the two distinct types of activities—propagation of Birsa's ideas (which he called 'scattering the seeds') forming the basis of the religious revitalization movement and the specific political mobilization.

Regarding the question whether Birsa's attitude to the traditional Munda culture perceptibly changed during the period between the first and the second movement, K.S. Singh noted a change,

> In its socio-cultural aspects it (the Birsa movement) graduated from reformative to a revivalistic phase closely linked with its political programme. In 1895, revivalism, if any, was only latent, in 1900 it came to the surface—the ancient 'ingredients' were restored to the people, the alien elements were to be weeded out and the racial enemies, both temporal and religious, expelled. The early emphasis on 'religious means' gave way to the open espousal of violence as the means of the struggle.[48]

Singh's view needs to be examined. 'Expulsion of racial enemies' was far from a revivalistic slogan. It had inspired the Munda resistance movement since the beginning. The 'ancient ingredients' with which Birsa wanted his followers to be familiar were, as revealed by contemporary official reports, just two temples, Chutia and Jagannathpur, and a fort, Naw Rattan. Sacred *tulsi* leaves were brought from the Chutia temple, sandal paste from Jagannathpur and sacred soil and water from a place near Naw Rattan. Songs, glorifying the heroic deeds of the Mundas in the revolt of 1831–2, were composed and collectively sung at the 'nocturnal gatherings of the Mundas'.

Apart from the songs, none of the 'ancient ingredients' formed any part of the old Munda culture. The two temples and the fort were not Munda creations at all. In fact, temple, in the sense of a place of worship having a distinctive architectural style, was alien to the Munda religious faith and rituals. The traditional place of Munda worship, known as the 'sacred grove', was an open space in the village, covered by a row of trees, and having no structure at all, except a big rough-hewn slab of stone at the foot of the trees. The Munda history which Birsa wanted the Mundas to become aware of was fictitious. Birsa's purpose in 'inventing the tradition' was to arouse in his followers a moral and spiritual fervour which would sustain them through the long and hard struggle against the enemy. He assured the Mundas that the *tulsi* leaves, sandal paste and the sacred soil and water would make them invulnerable to the superior might of the enemy. Whether or not Birsa wanted any other 'ancient ingredients' of Munda culture 'restored', there was scarcely any retreat from the meticulously planned religious revitalization, which aiming at reconstituting the Munda ethical and religious system, was inseparably linked with his political struggle. A change in Birsa's own religious faith may suggest a return to the Munda tradition. Christian Birsa's loyalty to the Christian faith greatly weakened, and his link with the church became tenuous. Though he did not formally sever the link, he preferred to be called 'Mundari Kol'. This, however, did not signify return to the Munda tradition. Birsa's distance from many aspects of this tradition indeed became largely unbridgeable. Worshipper of a personal God, he neither accepted the supreme God (*singbonga*) of the Mundas, nor the local gods (*bonga*). He publicly ridiculed all those august personalities of the Munda village who played a role in the ceremonies connected with the worship of these gods, such as the *pahan* (village priest), and persons recognized by the Munda village as having special powers of controlling the 'forces of evil', such as *mati*, *shoka* and *deonra*. The main strength of the Birsa movement was a community of followers unflinchingly loyal to his ideals of a new religion and a reconstituted political order.

In conclusion, it may be said that while Birsa scarcely ever retreated from the original ideals of 'religious revitalization', his political philosophy necessitated actions and use of symbols and myths which transcended the narrow limits of Hindu beliefs and rituals. The emergence of the Birsa sect as a result of this combination of religion and politics struck contemporaries like Hoffmann as a unique development in Munda society. He called the sect 'an entirely new caste of more than Hindu severity'. He described its nature and implications:

> This fact is more significant than may appear at first sight. For Mundas never did recognise separate castes, distinguishing between Munda and Munda. The only distinction of caste so far had been that which, under social penalties, separated the Munda from non-Mundas. It is really remarkable that this man [Birsa] and his clique should, within the last year and a half, had succeeded in creating a distinct caste of Mundas, who absolutely refuse to have any intercourse not only with their ordinary tribesmen, but who will not so much as allow their non-Birsaite brothers or grown up children to eat with them or cross their threshold. The house of a Birsaite was declared absolutely sacred, and no non-Birsaite was for any reason to cross it. I know personally of cases in which parents, visited by grown up children [presumably Birsaites], refused to admit them, and, contented themselves with handing uncooked food to them, which they might cook and eat anywhere they might please outside the parental house.

Compared to the Mundas the Oraons came under Hindu influence earlier, though this influence was perhaps negligible before the eighteenth century. Here, again, the crucial agency in its spread was the sect of itinerant Vaishnavas, locally called Bhagats. As in the Munda country, its remarkable expansion was directly correlated to the growth of the Oraon resistance to alien enemies particularly the Tana Bhagat movement (1914–22). The nature of Hindu influence on Oraon society in the two phases—before and after the beginning of the Tana movement (1914)—seems to have been misjudged by two well-known scholars: Risley dealing with the pre-Tana phase and Sarat Chandra Roy mainly with the Tana movement. Risley did not observe any novelty in the Bhagat phenomenon, and mixes it up with the traditional Oraon religious beliefs and practices. Roy regarded the Tana Bhagat movement as a mere continuation of the earlier Bhagat cult, characterizing it merely as a religious movement and denying any causal link whatsoever with the Oraon political aspirations at the time.

Roy has convincingly refuted Risley, who apparently confused a Bhagat with the traditional Oraon diviner (*mati*), both supposedly possessing spiritual powers. The confusion was perhaps not unnatural in view of the association of some prominent Bhagats, at one stage of their lives, with the usual art and practices of a *mati*. Even Jatra Bhagat, the founder of the Tana movement, had harboured, early in his life, an ambition to become an *Ojha* or a *mati*. However, a Bhagat was far from being identical with a *mati*. The difference between them is related to the source of their alleged spiritual powers. Roy called a Bhagat 'white magician' representing beneficent powers and a *mati* representing the forces of evil, the 'evil eye' and the 'evil mouth' of the Oraon tradition. A *mati* acquired his powers by practising 'magic art', through magic spells or *mantrams*, even seeking for the purpose the help of an evil spirit, cajoled into his service through the promise of an offer of human or other animal blood. A Bhagat normally avoided mediumistic and other occult practices, and believed to have acquired his powers from the grace of Mahadeo (Mahadeva, a Hindu God). The grace came hardly unasked for, it invariably called for a rigorous spiritual discipline, involving long hours of deep meditation. The spiritual powers thus acquired had to be preserved through similarly rigorous daily practices and observance of rules of ceremonial purity, such as leading a life of active devotion, abstinence from sex, from eating meat, except that of goat, from drinking liquor, and avoidance of dining with people addicted to drinking. Risley also erroneously attributed to Bhagats certain rituals usually followed by *matis*, such as offering sacrifices to the dreaded Goddess Kali (while a Bhagat's God was Mahadeo), sacrifices of pigs at funeral festivals, and of fowls over the graves of women dying shortly after childbirth. The Bhagat cult was thus a decisive break in the continuity of the Oraon tradition. The religious beliefs and practices of at least a few individuals were gradually tending from the polytheism of the Oraon religion to monotheism.

Roy's characterization of the Tana movement as a mere continuation of the earlier Bhagat cult ignores the strikingly novel elements in the movement. The Tana movement, partly based as it was on the Bhagat cult, differed from it in terms of its origins and orientation. The Bhagat cult was not a movement, but restricted to a few individuals, often belonging to specific families. Marked off from the rest of Oraon society, they cared little for converting other Oraons to this new faith and the new way of life. In fact, the extreme rigour characterizing a Bhagat's life precluded the growth of this elite group. At least one Bhagat sect, *Bachhidan Bhagat* (literally meaning 'calf giving Bhagats', i.e. those usually obliged to offer calves to their gurus on certain religious occasions), was presumably composed of relatively wealthy Oraons. In fact, Hindu influence was most marked among them. The Gosains, accepted by the sect as its gurus, were 'either degraded Brahmans or in some cases *Vaisnav-Vairagis* belonging to lower Hindu castes who periodically visit the Ranchi district from Gaya or Sahabad. . . .'[49] On the other hand, the new Tana movement was essentially a collective enterprise, a popular movement, aiming at the cultural and moral regeneration of the entire Oraon race. The leaders insisted on the transmission of their 'message of truth' to as many Oraons as possible, and great care was exercised in selecting the right kind of people for the purpose. The new movement necessarily set itself broader objectives than the earlier Bhagat cult. The means for realizing the objectives were also different. The Tana songs collected by Roy best indicate how the leaders conceived and planned the spiritual and moral regeneration of the tribe as a collectivity. Two major strands in their thinking are: (1) conception of a 'true religion', notion of a Supreme God, giver of 'knowledge' and 'wise speech', on whom the followers of the Tana precepts would constantly meditate, and (2) a ruthless rejection (*tana*, pulling down) of many of the earlier Oraon beliefs, rituals, practices and customs.

Such a broad-based movement was inconceivable in the eighteenth century. Roy has failed to explain why the emphasis in the Tana philosophy, at a specific point of time, on the cultural regeneration of the entire Oraon society, coincided with their large-scale resistance movement. He has denied any causal link between the two phenomena, though he has acknowledged the role in it of the deepening economic crisis at the time (partly crisis due to the sudden spurt in commodity prices during the First World War). He has concluded: 'Thus the social and economic aspects of this movement unfortunately came to be bound up with its religious aspects, to the prejudice of both.'[50] Curiously enough, what seemed to Roy an 'unfortunate' blend of religion and politics was precisely the distinguishing mark of the Tana movement. Whether it was harmful for both the religion and politics of the Oraons is not a worthwhile enquiry. All evidence suggests that the blending of the two enriched both.

A narrative of the Tana movement lies outside the scope of this essay.[51] Nevertheless; a brief discussion would help one to understand how the radical political temper of the Oraons tended to transform the character of the earlier Bhagat tradition bearing a strong Hindu influence. Initially, it was a revitalization movement of a pacifist sort. The pacifism had much to do with the disastrous outcome of the violent Birsa movement (1899–1900), which the Oraons had joined. The main emphasis thereafter was on the restoration of what the Oraons called their 'true religion' (*Kuruk Dharm*), purged of the impurities which, they believed, had crept into it because of their contacts with other tribal groups, particularly the Munda. However, it developed into an agrarian movement of a millenarian type during the 1914–22 period. The three new features of the Tana revitalization movement were the emphasis on the complete dissociation from the worship of *bhuts* (spirits) as being incompatible with the new notion of one God, the collective exorcism of *bhuts* from all parts of the Oraon country through incantation of divine *mantras* (holy words) taught by Jatra Bhagat, and the unprecedented comprehensiveness of the definition of 'unclean' practices and rituals to be jettisoned by the Oraons. The radical political tone of the movement became increasingly clear over time. Like Birsa, Jatra Bhagat claimed divine authority to call upon the Oraons to reconstruct their society and culture by purging it of all evils. He was also inspired by the vision of building a new world, completely different from the irredeemably corrupt one of the time. Like Birsa, he assured his followers that he would lead the exodus to the world of bliss. Initially, he wanted his followers to avoid any conflict with the enemies. The only 'political' programme in the movement forbade the Oraons to work as *dhangars* (day labourers). The programme became increasingly radicalized. The 'no rent' campaign and the 'land grab' movement, though generally localized, were aimed at attacking the alien domination over the Oraon villages. The public pronouncements of the leaders about the imminence of the '*Angrej Raj*' amounted to a questioning of the legitimacy of the colonial state. The 'religious' movement also continued with the same earnestness and moral fervour as earlier. As in the case of the Mundas, here too, the obvious Hindu influence on the 'religious' movement seldom led to any articulation of the Tanas with the Hindu religious establishment, and the hierarchical social organization. The Oraon religious movement, as noted earlier, was primarily a search for the roots of the *Kuruk Dharm*, the lapse from which, the Tanas believed, had led to their material distress and moral degradation. Adopting a few Hindu beliefs and rituals did not amount to an acceptance of the model of the Hindu social organization. Hindu Brahmins were never permitted any role in the Oraon religious and social ceremonies. The practice of wearing the sacred thread, perhaps more widespread here than in Munda society, had nothing to do with the idea of stratified ritual ranking. Two things are notable here. Unlike in Hindu society, 'there is no special ceremony of investiture of the sacred thread except that the name of *Bhagwan* [God] is taken while putting it on'. Second, as the Tanas themselves said, 'the sacred thread is the distinctive mark of the [Tana] Bhagat as the white flag which most Tanas set up in front of their houses is the distinctive mark of a [Tana] Bhagat's house'.[52]

The Oraon sentiments of solidarity and consciousness of identity survived despite the weakening of the organized Tana movement. This is evident from their cold attitude toward the efforts of the Arya Samaj, a Hindu organization, and of 'official Hinduism' to bring the Oraons into the Hindu fold. Roy was given the reasons for this by the Oraon leaders. One reason was the 'Oraon's suspicion of political or other motives at the back of such propaganda' of the Hindu organizations.

> On the other hand, enlightened leaders among the Oraons naturally fight shy of such propagandists under the reasonable apprehension that orthodox official Hinduism with the religious and social exclusiveness of the twice-born castes, would relagate the aboriginal converts to a very low, if not the lowest, stratum in the hierarchy of Hindu castes.[53]

In fact, the Arya Samaj did not practise what it preached: 'in theory it ignores all distinctions of caste . . . practice in this respect would appear to lag behind precept among most local *Arya Samajists*'.

The religious revitalization movement of the Ho can be divided into two distinct phases—1907 and 1931–2. The first, presumably influenced by the Munda movement, was largely confined to the 'villages round about the Chaibasa town', the major town of Singhbhum. The second, originating in Singhbhum, quickly spread over a vast area.

The Ho movement did not essentially differ from that elsewhere in the adivasi world. Some of its features are notable: (1) The more marked influence of the wider freedom struggle on the Ho region may have affected the 'purification' movement here. However, this did not happen. The trends in the Ho movement were largely determined by the existing Ho culture itself and only marginally affected by Gandhi's social and cultural programmes. The enthusiastic response of the Ho to his temperance movement was largely due to the crucial position of the Ho 'purification' movement in their vision of creating an independent polity of their own. (2) Despite the nearly identical objectives of the purification movements in different parts of the adivasi world, the nature of the old practices and rituals which the leaders wanted their followers to abandon was far from identical. For instance, there is a striking difference between the Birsa movement and the second phase of the Ho movement. Birsa entirely ignored the supreme God of the Mundas (*singbonga*), all the local gods (*bonga*), and also the traditional mode of worship at the 'sacred grove' (*sarna*) of the village. The idea of the sacred grove was fully restored in the Ho movement. The observance of 'purificatory' rites by the Ho was often followed by taking a dip in local rivers and visits to the *sarna*. More significantly, the *sarna* became associated with the growing consciousness of solidarity among the tribals. A religious practice and ritual followed by the Ho villages individually, was now transformed into a supra-village symbol—the symbol of a new perception of an underlying unity of the widely dispersed adivasi communities. The concept of the *sarna* became a construct used for uniting the tribal groups. 'Sarna Dharm' was the name used to denote the ancient religion of Chotanagpur tribals. (3) Whatever the attempts at the level of the movement's leadership to restore the old sacred institutions, the Ho, by about the time of second movement, had lost much of their reverence for many of their traditional institutions mainly as a result of the weakening of the tribal village organization. This partly accounted for the fact that the kind of 'social division' that developed, in both the Munda and Oraon societies, between the hard core of the 'purified' and the vacillating group, was relatively less pronounced in Ho society.

A near contemporary official document[54] is the main source of knowledge of the first Ho movement (1907), referred to as the 'starting' of 'a new religion'. The narrative points both to Hindu influence on the movement and to its limitation. While the concept of God in the new religion revealed the influence of abstract metaphysical Hindu thought, the religion wholly ignored the popular Hindu beliefs and practices. The followers of the new religion, called by its founder *Singrai Ho Satya* or *Punya Dharam* (a true or holy religion), worshipped only one invisible and omnipotent God whom they address as *Sat Malik* or True Lord. They had no image or representation of their God. On the other hand, 'they denounce the idolatory of the Hindus. They worship Him by means of *dhyan* or *jap* or meditation and devotion'. Though the document mentioned that 'they put on sacred threads like the Hindu Brahmans', it is not certain whether the Ho wearing the thread claimed a higher ritual status. Their break with much of the Ho tradition was as far-reaching as in the case of Munda and Oraon societies. 'They have given up all the dancings and observances of the Hos. They have given up the drinking of *Diang* or rice beer and are pure vegetarians. . . . They observe many other ceremonies and have fixed rules for the daily conduct of their lives even to the minutest details.'

The second movement, the Haribaba movement (1931–2), so named because its founder, Duka, called himself Haribaba, spread over wider area. A decisive factor was the stimulus provided by the freedom struggle at the time. The Ho had learnt of Gandhi's charismatic leadership earlier in 1925, when he had visited Chaibassa. For the Ho, Gandhi symbolized an alternative social and political order to the British Raj. The Ho leaders then publicly announced the end of this Raj, celebrating this august occasion with 'collective dancing and feasting', an invariable feature of their communal festivities. The colonial state's repression contained the anti-raj movement. Not much was heard of it till Duka launched his movement.[55]

In terms of purification, the Haribaba movement was even more wide-ranging than the Oraon Tana movement. Essentially an anti-*bonga* (spirit) movement, it had some peculiar features because of the specific local beliefs regarding the location of the *bongas* and *bhuts*, and the modalities of their worship. The *bhuts*, the Ho believed, preferred to hide themselves in the innermost recesses of houses and other places, and the best way to bring them out was to harass them by making prolonged loud and distracting noises, such as the incessant beating of drums. Black was the colour the Ho associated with the *bongas*. Anything black had to be thrown out. 'All black domestic animals like black goats, black chickens etc. were driven out of the village into the forest. They were suspected of being the abode of evil spirits.' Anyone keen on joining the movement had to take a solemn oath to expel the *bongas*, and also to 'throw out of his house all the *agam tapan* objects i.e. objects kept as outward signs of some promises made usually to malign spirits to perform certain sacrifices upon receiving some specific favour'. Practices connected with the art of 'black magic' were strictly forbidden. 'All the *najoms* (objects used for poisoning the enemy) and *chuka* (earthen vessels used for divination) kept in their houses had to be thrown out.' Like the Santal Kherwars, Birsaite Mundas and Tana Bhagats, Haribaba's disciples constantly preached against the evil of witchcraft.

Following the eradication of the *bhuts* and *bongas* in these various ways, the disciples had to perform other purification rites, such as bathing in the local rivers and visiting the sacred grove (*sarna*) of the village; they were expected to carry two things for worship at the grove: sundried rice and vermilion. The rice sanctified by the guru was returned to them. The sacred water (*got da*) which the guru sprinkled on them, according to the Ho, produced in them trance-like feelings.

As elsewhere, the reform programme was fairly demanding. However, Haribaba might not have faced the same opposition to his reforms from the conservative section of Ho society as leaders of reform movements among the Santal, the Munda and the Oraon did. A contemporary report on Ho society and culture in the government estate Kolhan in the second decade of the twentieth century reveals that the Ho had by then lost much of their old reverence for their sacred traditions and institutions, the two traditions specifically mentioned were the Ho burial custom and the attitude toward the trees of the 'sacred grove'.[56] An old Ho burial custom (also observable among the Munda), called *Jangtopa*, was to bring the bones of a Ho buried anywhere outside his ancestral village to the village, and to bury them in the communal graveyard there, invariably in the presence of the other villagers. The burial place was marked by a large piece of flat stone (*sasandiri*). The practice, signifying that the burial was not just a family affair, was one of the village's sacred ceremonies. The custom, at the time the official observed it, largely ceased to be communal and sacred. As indicated by the report, the change was not merely the result of a change in cultural values:

> . . . nowadays, this old custom is being given up and the body itself is buried [not burnt]. This is due in part to the denudation of the village forests and the consequent difficulty to procure wood to burn the body. Formerly there was only one *sasan* or burial ground for the members of one *killi* [clan] in each village, but nowadays with the disintegration of the village communal systems, each family or household is making a separate

sasan of its own, and the *sasan* or burial ground is a corner of the very courtyard. . . . The former reverence for the *sasandiri* [the flat stone placed on the burial place] is also passing away and with the custom of making *sasans* in the courtyards, they are being used now as seats, where a man can play, sleep, or as grinding stones and without any apparent thought of the things buried underneath.

The old attitude to the trees of the sacred grove [*sarna, Jahira*] also noticeably changed. The communal ban on felling them tended to be violated. The *Jahiras* are the sacred grove of the Hos and formerly no Ho would dare to cut even a branch or use the wood for his household and other domestic purposes, but nowadays the respect due to the abodes of their *bongas* is dying out. The *Jahiras* are the only places where very old trees, the remnants of the original forestclad tracts, are to be found, and the trees were preserved because no Ho would dare to cut a tree without exciting the wrath of its spiritual residents. But during the settlement proceedings [1913–18] it was noticed that the trees had been skinned off, so that trees may die and the villagers be able to appropriate the dry wood without being accused by the local authorities of having felled live trees.

Whether the 'purified' Ho tended to be integrated into the Hindu caste system is relevant to the theme of this essay. It would be in order to examine in this connection a point of view[57] emphasizing the influence of the model of the Hindu caste system on the Haribabaites. Two instances of this influence, based on a contemporary official report, have been cited. First, Harima, Haribaba's wife, used to sprinkle holy water (*Haripani*) on the followers in order to 'raise' them to 'some sort of *jat* [caste]', i.e. to a higher rank in the caste system. Second, in the earlier stages Haribaba preached traditional purity and racial isolation. He wanted his followers to have nothing to do with Tantis, the weaver caste and others, whom they considered as inferior people.[58]

The first instance seems inconclusive. What Harima precisely meant by 'raising' the persons who visited her to some sort of '*jat*' remains vague. Even the official report on the practice was unsure of its implications in terms of any positional change in the caste system. 'Where they [the persons receiving *Haripani*] stand with the Hindus is still a matter of conjecture.' The intolerance of the *Tantis* (weavers) may of course be differently explained. It had much to do with the rapid change in the *recent* years in their traditional role in the Ho village economy in the context of the increasing involvement of Ho villages in the wider market economy. Earlier the Ho villages, largely isolated from the money-based economy of the neighbourhood, solely depended on the *Tantis*, a migrant group long settled in the village, for the supply of cloth. This was the reason why the Ho regarded the *Tantis*, despite being aliens generally distrusted by them, as a part of the village community. The spread of the market system substantially altered this traditional role of the *Tantis*. The new role was one of an acquisitive community of cloth merchants doing business all for the sake of profit. An official report (1897)[59] described this changed role of the *Tantis* in the government estate of Kolhan, especially the various sources of their power in the village.

> The Tanti population . . . is now scattered over the Kolhan. The coarse cloths worn by the people in the Kolhan is almost entirely manufactured by the people of this caste, who live for the most part on the proceeds derived from this source. A large number have, however, taken to the cultivation of land. They are shrewd and full of intrigue, and have acquired considerable influence in the Kol communities. The village accountants or *tahsildars* and *dakuas* or village watchmen are almost invariably of this caste. A Tanti is the legal adviser of the villagers, no suit or litigation being entered on without his opinion being taken. They exercise a most mischievous influence in the kol villages, and are about the most obnoxious class of foreigners. In my opinion no Tanti should be allowed to be either *tahsildar* or *dakua* in the Kolhan.

It is little wonder that Haribaba cautioned his followers about the *Tantis*, 'shrewd and full of intrigue', 'the most obnoxious class of foreigners in the Kol villages', and exercising 'a most mischievous influence' in the villages. His advice to his disciples to keep away from these wily *Tantis*, denounced by him as 'inferior people', had therefore nothing to do with the emulation of the Hindu caste model. The Haribabaites, despite the obvious Hindu influence on them, were just 'purified' Ho, deeply attached to their culture, now considerably purged of many of its 'unclean' elements.

Some professional anthropologists like Martin Orans, Sarat Chandra Roy,[60] Nirmal Kumar Bose and Surajit Sinha have expressed their views on the question of the so-called 'Hinduization' of adivasis. Two broad trends are observable in their studies. Roy and Orans have discussed at length the question of the relevance of adivasi politics of their 'new religion'. Bose and Sinha have ignored this relationship in their study of Hindu influence on adivasis.

Part of Orans' argument, particularly his idea of 'rank concession syndrome', has been examined earlier. My disagreement with him is basic. While he delinks Santal politics from their new religious movement (Kherwar movement), I have argued that the Santal social and religious reform movement is not at all intelligible outside the context of the political radicalism of the Santal at the time. Another aspect of his view also needs to be reconsidered. He characterized an outcome of Hindu influence on the Santal as a kind of reshaping of the 'Little Tradition' of the Santal on the model of the 'Great Tradition', in this case the Hindu tradition. The 'Great Tradition' has been defined as one 'having the qualities of explicitness, systematization and reflectiveness', and the 'Little Tradition' has been 'conceived of as product of folk societies and as relatively lacking in these qualities'.[61]

However, the emulation of the Great Tradition primarily related to form, not content. The Santal tradition itself was not replaced, but enriched. In fact, Orans' own argument leads to this conclusion:

> Having taken much from these neighbours [Hindus], but desirous of maintaining their identity, they [the Santal] decided to create a 'great tradition' of their own rather than accept the one belonging to their neighbours. There is, for example, an attempt to codify Santal traditions in writing and the development of a distinctive script in which to record these traditions. In place of an essentially inexplicit religious ideology expressed in ritual, there is the development of an explicit religious ideology with an emphasis on morality. There is also the elaboration of literary forms wholly unlike the unpretentious traditional ones.

The Santal grove, a place of collective worship, was perceived as an organized institution, like the Hindu temple. The Santal language had no name for Santal religion. They now called it *Sarna Dharam*, meaning thereby an explicitly codified set of religious beliefs, like Hinduism.[62] The point to be debated is whether the changes in the Santal culture which Orans has identified—attempts at codification of the Santal traditions in writing, development of a script, the idea of *Sarna Dharam*, etc.,—were actually the results of the conscious attempt of the Santals to reconstruct their Little Tradition on the model of the Great Hindu Tradition. The changes had presumably much to do with the kind of 'organized politics', distinguishable from the earlier organization of the Santal resistance, that developed since the 1930s.

It is clear from the study of the Tana Bhagat movement that Roy has completely misjudged its nature, particularly the nature of the integral relationship between the organized Oraon resistance movement and the new Tana religion. His characterization of the Birsa movement is equally misleading. He went even further to conclude that the motivating force behind Birsa's new religion was just his personal ambition.[63] In the study of the movement presented in this essay, I have emphasized two things: the influence of the near contemporary Kherwar religious revitalization movement, and more importantly, Birsa's vision of creating an independent Munda polity based on the loyalty of a 'purified' Munda community, his religion prescribing precisely the requirements of this purification.

Nirmal Kumar Bose has presented his arguments in a celebrated paper 'The Hindu Method of Tribal Absorption'[64] and in his *Hindu Samajer Garan* (1949) (translated into English by Andre Beteille).[65] The form of the 'Hindu method of tribal absorption' differed in the two cases studied by him—the Juang of Orissa and the Munda-Oraon of Bihar.

In the first case, the 'absorption' was initially primarily economic in nature.[66] The unviability, for various reasons, of shifting cultivation, the traditional mode of Juang subsistence, forced them

to adopt wet cultivation in the valleys between the hills. They also work in bamboo and sell baskets, wicker-boxes and winnowing fans to the neighbouring people, and with the money earned in this way they buy cloth and salt or iron and rice when they do not grow the latter. Thus, instead of being economically more or less self-contained, they have now been tagged on to the larger body of Hindu society; they now form only one cog in the wheel of the advanced productive machinery.

Emulation by the Juang of Hindu cultural traits resulted from 'this fact of economic affiliation to Hindu society'. Why did this emulation take place at all? Bose has assumed its automaticity in the context of the 'economic affiliation'. The Juang look upon 'Hindu culture as superior to their own. . . . In the science of Physics, we are told that electricity flows from high potential to low; and in culture also it seems to flow from an economically dominant group to a poorer one when the two are tied together to form a larger productive organization. . . .' Why did the Juang, now practically a part of the Hindu social organization occupying, like many other *jatis*, a lowly position in the Hindu caste hierarchy, generally not contest the Hindu cultural symbols? Bose has explained it thus:

> the subjugated classes did not rise in revolt, because Hindu society assured to them a certain minimum of economic security which they could not attain under their own tribal productive system. . . . The Hindus, moreover, exercised a policy of *laissez faire* with regard to the social and religious practices of tribal peoples even when they came within Hinduism, and this cultural autonomy may partly have been responsible for keeping the subjugated tribes satisfied, and also for taking the edge off their discontent to a certain extent.

In the case of the Munda-Oraon, the method of 'tribal absorption' was different. Its background, Bose has argued, was the rise in this society of numerous 'service groups', whom the Munda-Oraon, as controllers of the village land, treated as socially inferior. In the context of the 'pressure of an immigrant population', the Mundas, 'seeing the possibility of rising levels of living by adopting the kind of division of labour which prevailed in the Braminical society . . . began to imitate some of their crafts'.[67] For instance, 'They learnt to sow cotton and make yarn with a spinning wheel; they gave up their plank press and adopted the more elaborate oilpress of the *Kolus*. But because the Kolus were rated low in Hindu society, for fear of losing caste the Mundas worked the new oil press not by bullocks but with the labour power of their own woman folk.' Bose has drawn the following inference from this development: 'the productive organization which was developed in Hindu society on the basis of a close association between different castes came to be accepted by the Mundas, and just as Hindu society displays gradations among the different castes, so also distinctions between the high and the low came to be established'. The descendants of the founders of Munda-Oraon villages 'refused to recognise as their equals those families which lived only by blacksmithery or weaving or tending cattle'. As a result, 'when along with the productive organization of Brahminical society, social gradations also became pervasive among the Kol speaking communities, they became transformed for all practical purposes into a constituent community of Hindu society',[68] because 'in surrendering themselves to the productive arrangements of Brahminical society, they tacitly accepted the caste system and the *Varna* creed'.[69] 'The spread of Brahminical influence', in forms other than the 'acceptance' of the varna system, also gradually occurred, partly as a result of considerable Brahmin settlements, which the Hinduized royal family had consistently encouraged. In fact, Bose has concluded that compared to Juang society 'the influence of the Aryan or Brahminical influence over the Mundas and the Oraons was greater in extent and depth'.[70]

Surajit Sinha in his paper 'State Formation and Rajput Myth in Tribal Central India',[71] has argued, mainly with reference to the Bhumij tribe of Burrabhum, how 'state formation and the associated creation of a myth of Rajput ancestry provided a stratified structural base for integration of tribes with the social organization of Indian civilization'.[72] As a result of the state formation 'the traditional segmentary clan-territory units of the tribal Bhumij were reorganized into a hierarchic feudal state with a Raja of a pargana, claiming Rajput-Kshatriya status at the top having control over the lower orders of chiefs. Roughly corresponding to the feudal hierarchy there was a socio-ritual status hierarchy of endogamous grades. . ...' A development related to the process of state formation was the emergence of petty landed interests outside the framework of the traditional land system:

numerous immigrant Brahmins received land grants from the royal family. The Brahmins 'provided the tribal chieftain with prestigious myths and ritual symbols in support of their Rajput status'.[73]

Sinha's view will be examined here, partly because he has pointed out important qualifications of his central argument. In fact, as has been mentioned elsewhere, earlier studies of the alleged 'transformation' of the Bhumij tribe into 'caste' clearly noted that the process mostly affected the top echelons of the emerging power hierarchy in the Bhumij territory. Sinha has reached the same conclusion:

> It should be made clear . . . that the tribals at the lower rungs of the social hierarchy were only feebly touched by the aspiration for identification as Rajput-Kshatriyas. Their poor economic position, more than any other factor, virtually ruled out the possiblility of ever realizing the status of Rajput for which it is essential to 'purchase' the ritual services of Brahmins of the right kind. There is also the fact that the Rajputized chieftains used to maintain a fairly close control over the inter-ethnic rank hierarchy in their respective territories. The various tribes and castes, in their turn, were ever watchful over possible supersession of rank claims by the groups which were traditionally considered relatively low. This partially explains the fact that the tribes and castes living within the territory of a Rajputized chieftain were able to maintain their respective ethnic identities through centuries instead of rapidly melting into monolithic Rajput affiliation. Thus, while the emergent structure facilitated the upper hierarchies to attain Rajput status, the power of the same structure was directed, to a considerable extent, toward inhibiting the realization of similar aspirations by commoners.[74]

This conclusion applies to Bose's study as well. The so-called 'spread of Brahminical influence' in the Munda-Oraon country was primarily confined to the new ruling groups, i.e. the royal family and its beneficiaries. The royal family had never shown any interest in popularizing the 'royal religion' among the common tribals. In fact, the increasing bitterness of tribal villages toward the royal family and its assorted dependents inevitably checked any possible diffusion of Brahminical influence. 'As a result, in spite of their progressive integration with Hindu society and culture, the Mundas, in common with many other Kolarian tribes of Chotanagpur, maintain a residual feeling of separation and antagonism about the Hindu *Dikku*' (foreigners).[75]

Bose's analysis of the implications of the development of 'service groups' in the Munda-Oraon society in terms of the articulation of the tribal villages with the 'productive organization of Brahminical society' and the wider Hindu caste organization is of doubtful validity. The dependence of the tribal village for some services, which could not be wholly provided internally does point to a link with the wider economic system. But there was nothing particularly Hindu about the availability of the services. Part of Bose's argument rests on the assumption that the inferior social status of the artisan groups in general in Munda-Oraon society was a direct outcome of the 'tacit acceptance of the caste system and the varna creed'. It is notable that not just artisan groups, but even tribal cultivators of other villages (*eta hanaranka*) were similarly treated as economically and socially inferior, unless they were admitted to the tribal village organization after the performance of some formal ceremonies. This was one of the means of preserving the control of the descendants (in the male line) of the family of village founders (*khutkathidars*) over village resources. The tribal feeling of exclusiveness had other dimensions too. For instance, marrying outside the 'tribe' and within a clan was considered a serious offence. Tribals believed that violation of the norm undermined the stability of their village.

It may be argued that the greater degree of integration of Juang society into the more advanced economic organization in the neighbourhood (not necessarily Hindu) was primarily because of the unstable base of their earlier mode of subsistence, shifting cultivation, particularly when the Juang population increased or encroachments on their land by outsiders limited their options regarding the choice of the area for the next shift in cultivation. The Juang village organization was inevitably much weaker than the tribal village organization in zones of settled agriculture, and its limited solidarity made it more vulnerable to alien cultural influences. This was also applicable to settled agriculturists such as the Santal and the Munda-Oraon, when, for various reasons, they became segregated from their traditional villages.

In conclusion, the major arguments presented here may be summarized: (1) Increased Hindu cultural influences on the adivasis did not invariably necessitate their articulation with the caste-based and hierarchical Hindu social organization. (2) The usual representations of the 'Hinduization' process tended to ignore the will and subjectivity of the adivasi groups emulating Hindu beliefs and practices. A crucial determinant of this will and subjectivity was the increasing radicalization of the adivasi protest movements. (3) Integration into the Hindu social organization was conditional on the nature of the countervailing process, i.e. adivasi society's will and efforts to maintain its identity. The integration was easier where the opposite force was weak or non-existent. (4) Even where integration did not occur, emulation of Hindu traits generally implied a narrowing of the distance between the Hindu and adivasi cultural traditions. This is what resulted from the interaction of the Great and the Little Traditions. Orans' conclusion is worth quoting:

> Paradoxically, while these developments involve rejection of numerous Hindu practices, they introduce fundamental beliefs and values of Hinduism which previously had made hardly any progress among the Santal. Thus, while distinctive traits are re-emphasized, the configurations and orientation of Santal culture become somewhat more like those of the Hindus.

NOTES

1. H.H. Risley, *The Tribes and Castes of Bengal*, vol.1, *Introductory Essay*, Calcutta: Bengal Secretariat Press, 1891, I will say more about the instances in my examination of Risley's arguments.
2. *The People of India*, London, 1915, 2nd edn., New Delhi: Oriental Books, 1969, p. 72.
3. G.S. Ghurye, *The Aborogines-so-called and Their Future*, Pune: Gokhale Institute of Politics and Economics, 1943.

4. This concept has been discussed at length later.
5. Surajit Sinha, *Tribes and Indian Civilization: Structures and Transformations*, Varanasi: N.K. Bose Memorial Foundation, 1981, p. 9.
6. K.S. Singh, *Tribal Society in India*, New Delhi: Manohar, 1985, Chap. 5; 'Tribalization'.
7. Ibid., p. 88. Of the incoming communities appreciably affected by the local tribal culture reference may be to the artisans. The length of their stay in the tribal village and the indispensability of their role in the tribal village economy made them an inseparable part of the village life.
8. E. Lister, *Bihar and Orissa District Gazetteers, Hazaribagh*, Patna: Bihar and Orissa Government Printing Press, 1917.
9. The relevant passages from Buchanan's *Bhagalpur Journal* (the journal he maintained during his tour of the district) are quoted in H. McPherson, *Final Report on the Survey and Settlement Operations in the Santal Parganas*, Calcutta: Bengal Secretariat Book Depot, 1909, para 21.
10. Bengal Judicial Criminal Proceedings, 31 March 1834, no. 51; Joint Commissioners of Jungle Mehals to the Secretary to the Government, Judicial Dept., Government of Bengal, dated 4 September 1833; paras 3-5 of the report.
11. I have elaborated the argument in my paper 'Towards an Understanding of the Tribal World of Colonial Eastern India', in S. Taniguchi, H. Yanagisawa, T. Shinoda and F. Oshikawa, eds., *Economic Changes and Social Transformation in Modern and Contemporary South Asia*, Tokyo: Hitotsubashi University, 1994, Section 2.
12. E.T. Dalton, *Descriptive Ethnology of Bengal*, 1st edn., Calcutta: Government Printing Press, 1872, rpt. 1960 and 1973, Calcutta, Firma KL Mukhopadhyay.
13. Bengal Judicial Proceedings, November 1874, nos. 1–3.
14. Ibid.
15. Bengal General (Misc.) Proceedings, September 1875, File no. 133–1/4.
16. Bengal Judicial Proceedings, March 1875.
17. Ibid., File no. 40–88.
18. Ibid., File no. 40–89.
19. Bengal Judicial Proceedings, August 1881, nos. 39–40.
20. *Asiatic Studies*, 1st edn., London, 1882, p. 102; cited in H.H. Risley, *Tribes and Castes of Bengal*, vol. 1, 'Introductory Essay', p. iii.
21. Quoted in Risley, *Tribes and Castes*, vol. 1, 'Introductory Essay', p. iii.
22. Dalton, *Descriptive Ethnology*, rpt., Calcutta, 1960, pp. 171–5.
23. H.H. Risley, *Special Note on Burrabhum*, Calcutta, 1883; *Tribes and Castes*

and *The People of India*. Risley has evidently heavily drawn from Dalton. Some of his observations are, however, based on his own investigation, mainly in the 1880s, which are contained in the essay 'Bhumij', in *Tribes and Castes.*

24. Risley, *Tribes and Castes*, vol. 1, p. 117.
25. Ibid., pp. 117–18.
26. Ibid., pp. 124–5.
27. Ibid., 'Introductory Essay', pp. xv–xviii.
28. Ibid., pp. xvii–xviii.
29. The official reports on which my study of the movement is mostly based are included in the following archival records: Bengal Judicial Proceedings, November 1874, March 1875 and August 1881.
30. O'Malley's account, written around 1910 and based on 'accounts given by Santals at the present time', grossly misrepresented the crucial feature of the movement—religious revitalization. Bhagirath, the leader of the movement in 1874, appears in this account as a downright imposter, pursuing purely selfish aims and cunningly exploiting the credulity of simpleminded Santals. L.S.S. O'Malley, *Bihar District Gazetteers, Santal Parganas*, Calcutta: Bengal Secretariat Book Depot, 1910, pp. 145–51.
31. Some of the teachings of the Vaishnavas, a Hindu sect, such as rejection of the hierarchial Hindu caste system and the emphasis on equality, love and brotherhood as the basis of an alternative social organization, must have impressed the Santals.
32. Such a guru, Kolean, confided in Skrefsrud, a Norwegian missionary, about the monotheistic element in the early Santal religious thought. Skrefsrud's work in Santali was translated by P.O. Bodding, *Traditions and Institutions of the Santals*, Oslo: A.W. Brag Boktry, 1942, p. 132. Santal society revered a guru partly because of his superior knowledge of the Santal oral tradition.
33. Bengal Judicial Proceedings, August 1881, nos. 39–41.
34. Martin Orans, *The Santal: A Tribe in Search of a Great Tradition*, Detroit: Wayne State University Press, 1965, pp. 33–9.
35. Bengal Judicial Proceedings, November 1874; nos. 1–3. Boxwell's report was dated 1 October 1874.
36. Bengal General Miscellaneous Proceedings, September 1875, *Bhagalpur Commissioner's Annual Report, 1874–5*, para 19.
37. Bengal Judicial Proceedings, August 1881, nos. 39–41, Appendix C.
38. Ibid., Bhagalpur Commissioner's letter of 8 June 1881, para 12.
39. 'Safai' meant the community of clean Santals. 'Babaji' was the name by

which the Vaishnava gurus were locally called. The words were not new. What was new was that they now denoted distinctive groups. Samra was a new group, named after Samra village in the Godda subdivision of the district of Santal Parganas.

40. J.H. Hutton, 'Primitive Tribes', in O'Malley, ed., *Modern India and the West*, 2nd edn., New Delhi: Oxford University Press, p. 437.
41. W.G. Archer, 'Tribal Law and Justice', in *A Report on the Santal*, New Delhi: Concept Publishing Company, 1984, pp. 655–6 (the manuscript of the book was completed in 1946).
42. K.S. Singh, *Birsa Munda and His Movement, 1874–1901: A Study of a Millenarian Movement in Chhotanagpur*, Calcutta: Oxford University Press, 1983, p. 41.
43. Bengal General Miscellaneous Proceedings, August 1881, nos. 5–8, para. 38 of the report.
44. Ibid., para. 192.
45. The Sardar movement, also known as *Mulki Larai*, continued for long (1858–94) and was primarily directed against the alien expropriators of their lands, in which they asserted a prescriptive status by virtue of their alleged descent from the families of the village founders.
46. Bengal General Miscellaneous Proceedings, November 1896, nos. 20–1, Chotanagpur Divisional Commissioners' Annual Report, 1895–6, para. 4.
47. In his letter (14 January 1900) to the Chotanagpur Commissioner, Father Hoffmann, a Catholic missionary, has described the activities of these preachers'. The *Puranakas*, presumably a small group composed of members 'picked out carefully all over the country' and closest to the leader Birsa, had access to the 'nocturnal meetings' deciding vital strategies of the 'political path'. They probably formed the hard core of the committed Birsaites, 'who never swerved from the original purpose of open revolt'. The *Nanakas*, the 'new members', 'were armed as well as the others; but it appears that they were not admitted to any important *panchayats* [group meetings where important decisions were made]. The practical resolutions were, however, communicated to them.' India Home Department Progs., August 1900, no. 335, Enclosure 4.
48. K.S. Singh, *The Dust Storm and the Hanging Mist: A Study of Birsa Munda and His Movement in Chhotanagpur (1874–1901)*, Calcutta: Firma KL Mukhopadhyay, 1966, p. 93.
49. S.C. Roy, *Oraon Religion and Customs*, Ranchi: Man in India Office, 1928, rpt., Calcutta, 1972, pp. 230–1.
50. Ibid., p. 247.

51. I have described this at considerable length in 'The Story of a Tribal Revolt in the Bengal Presidency: The Religion and Politics of the Oraons, 1900–26', in Adhir Chakravarti, ed., *Aspects of Socio-economic Changes and Political Awakening in Bengal*, Calcutta: West Bengal State Archives, 1989, pp. 30–57.
52. Roy, *Oraon Religion and Customs*, p. 290.
53. Ibid., p. 293.
54. Dahn Mashi Panna, Assistant Settlement Officer, Kolhan Government Estate, 'Notes on the Hos', in A.D. Tuckey, *Final Report on the resettlement of the Kolhan Government Estate in the District of Singbhum, 1913–1918*, Patna: Bihar and Orissa Government Printing, 1920, Appendix E. T.A. Craven, *Final Report on the Settlement of Kolhan Government Estate* (District of Singhbhum), Calcutta: Bengal Secretariat Press, 1898, para. 73.
55. An excellent study of the movement brings out its complexity, Mathew Areeparampil, 'Socio-cultural and Religious Movements among the Ho Tribals of Singbhum District of Bihar', in Mrinal Miri, ed., *Continuity and Change in Tribal Society*, Shimla: Indian Institute of Advanced Study, 1993.
56. See note 54.
57. See note 55, pp. 401–2.
58. Ibid., p. 399.
59. T.A. Craven, *Final Report on the Settlement of the Kolhan Estate in District Singhbhum in the Year 1897*, para. 73.
60. Roy was not, literally, a professional anthropologist. A lawyer by profession he developed a keen interest in the Bihar adivasi societies, and his researches have substantially enriched one's understanding of them.
61. Martin Orans, *The Santal: A Tribe in Search of a Great Tradition*, Detroit: Wayne State University Press, 1965, 'Introduction', p. ix.
62. Ibid., p. 105.
63. S.C. Roy, *The Mundas and Their Country*, Calcutta: City Book Society, 1912; rpt., Bombay: Asia Publishing House, 1950, pp. 187–97.
64. Originally published in *Science and Culture*, vol. VII, 1941, the essay was included in his collection of essays, Nirmal Kumar Bose, *Culture and Society in India*, Bombay: Asia Publishing House, 1967, Chap. XII.
65. Andre Beteille, *Structure of Hindu Society*, New Delhi: Orient Longman Limited, 1975.
66. N.K. Bose, 'The Hindu Method', in *Culture and Society in India*, Chap. XII, pp. 203–15. Bose did his field work here in 1928.
67. Beteille, *Structure of Hindu Society*, p. 56. Bose related the 'arrival of

many other castes, such as Cultivators, Carpenters, Blacksmiths, Barbers, Oilpressers, Bellmetal workers and so on' partly to the increasing consolidation of the powers of alien zamindars and *thikadars* [rent farmers], very many of whom were Hindus. Ibid., p. 54.

68. Ibid., pp. 46–7.
69. Ibid, p. 54.
70. Ibid., p. 71.
71. Surajit Sinha, 'State Formation and Rajput Myth in Tribal Central India', *Man in India*, Jan.–March 1962.
72. Sinha has briefly summarized the arguments of his paper in *Tribes and Indian Civilization*, Varanasi: N.K. Bose Memorial Foundation, 1981, pp. 7–8.
73. Ibid., p. 8. For an elaborate treatment of the theme, see Sinha, 'State Formation', pp. 70–9.
74. Sinha, ibid., pp. 76–7.
75. Ibid., pp. 77–8.

Reflections on the Concept of Regional History

Sabyasachi Bhattacharya

I have written about the concept of regional history in India earlier and I will draw upon my earlier writings and reflect upon the problem posed by this concept of regional history in the light of the historiography of a selected region. Those who are familiar with my earlier writings will kindly pardon me if they find a restatement irksome. I hope to be pardoned in view of the importance of the problem of regionalization in writing history, a problem connected with the far greater problem of regionalism in India's polity and society.

Apart from the importance of regionalization as a methodological problem in historiography, there is another reason why I chose this as the theme of my discourse. At one time, when government funding was not available because of the British Indian government's policy, small private associations in many parts of India played an important role in opening up archaeological and archival work connected with historical research and also in publishing journals. In social sciences, *Man in India* and the *Journal of Bihar and Orissa Research Society* readily come to mind; there were institutions in neighbouring Bengal such as the Varendra Research Society or the Bangiya Sahitya Parishad. All of these grew within the framework of small voluntary associations, limited to a region, and some of them grew beyond regional stature; their common feature was to establish a discourse of regional history well-founded in local research into documents, folklores, indigenous knowledge systems and tradition, social and cultural practices, family and caste histories, biographies of local notables, etc. In countries like England and France, a major part of historical research continues to emanate from such institutions. It is to be hoped that local institutional effort would supplement the writings which issue from metropolitan cities, national institutions and big commercial publishers. Regional research by local institutions may add a new dimension to knowledge of India's past.

I will begin with the proposition that historians talk about regions all the time but usually they do not give any thought to region as a concept. I have in mind here academic historians in the sphere of professional writing as distinct from some writers who use history to build regional sentiments for political purposes. Professional historians' writings would use regional categories without paying much attention to them for they are taken for granted. Some of these regions pertain to a particular period (e.g. the Bombay Presidency which was a colonial invention, without a past and wiped out as a category since independence). Some notions of regionalization have deep historical roots (e.g. Oudh of the British, preceded by Awadh of the medieval times, and in turn preceded by Ayodhya), though the spatial boundaries shifted. Sometimes historians also use a regional category by projecting backwards recently created political or administrative units (e.g. there are histories of Himachal Pradesh). Needless to say, the basis of regionalization is also diverse: regions may be defined culturally (such as Maha-Koshala, or Jharkhand), linguistically (e.g. the Bhojpuri region), in terms of administrative units (for instance Northern Circars of the Madras Presidency or any district of British India), according to ecological classification (such as the Gangetic delta), or ethnic identities (e.g. Nagaland).

What kind of systematic thinking has been devoted to regionalization, given this diversity and confusion? How do historians define regions? These are important questions because very often a mentality labelled 'regionalism' influences the public mind and claims authority from real or supposed historical evidence. Therefore, a great responsibility devolves upon historians and they need to examine the basis of regionalization. My argument will be that historians in a sense construct the 'region'. Therefore, it is important to deliberate at length on this than one is wont to do on account of one's tendency to take regions as 'given'.

It is fairly obvious from the examples cited here that what historians denote as regions are not immutable, that they originate in a particular period of history and may cease to be meaningful in another period. Thus, Oudh was a meaningful category up to its incorporation into British India, it ceased to be fully so since then. Likewise, the Bombay Presidency may have meant something in the nineteenth century gazetteers and histories, but it is scarcely a viable category before or after. And again, what were the limits of the region called Bengal depends on which century is being referred to (and, if I may suggest in jest, whether or not one is a Bengalee). Regions are therefore (except, of course, purely technically geographical ones) products of history. They are neither ephemeral nor unchanging and everlasting. Sometimes a kind of regional chauvinism may lead the layman to assume that they are everlasting but historians know how history in the long run makes and unmakes regions. Regions may arise and disintegrate, expand and contract. I am reminded here of Fernand Braudel's approach to the Mediterranean in defining 'a Mediterranean of historical dimension' he found that it expanded and contracted over time.

Second, the examples of regional categories cited earlier also show a diversity in the criteria of regionalization. Sometimes the criterion is linguistic, at other times it is political–administrative, or even communal, and so on. Joseph Schwartzberg, long before he became famous for his historical atlas of India, wrote a perceptive paper in 1967 on this issue.[1] As a social geographer, he distinguished three types of regionalization: (1) denoted, (2) instituted, and (3) 'naively given'. By 'denoted' region he meant regions which are distinguished and delimited with a particular purpose in view (of a linguist, or a historian, or an anthropologist) unrelated to the existing units for administrative purposes. The 'instituted' region, on the other hand, arises out of administrative functions, in order to facilitate the performance of and to define the spatial limits of such functions. Finally, the 'naively given' region is recognised as a meaningful territorial unit by the people who live there or by other people to whom it is of some concern, such as Saurashtra or Jharkhand.

This scheme enables one to think systematically about the criteria of regionalization. It is, of course, quite possible that a region may satisfy more than one criterion or purpose of regional delineation. For example, a 'naively given' region that is perceived as a unit by itself and others, may also be an administrative unit and or be denoted as a unit in linguistic or ethnic or communal terms. Evidently, in India linguistic reorganization and re-reorganization *ad infinitum*, since its acceptance by the Congress in the pre-independence period, has promoted trends towards the congruence of 'instituted' with 'naively given' regional boundaries, but the epistemological status of the 'naively given', instituted and denoted regions should be recognized as different.

Which of these types of regionalization schemes the historian should use would obviously depend upon his theme of research. For example, the instituted region would be appropriate if the historian is working in the political–administrative area; he would opt for the so-called 'naively given' region if he is dealing with social and cultural history. It is, however, the 'denoted' region which is the construct of scholarly work. The historian may begin with given regions according to folk perception or administrative fiat, but he arrives at a pattern of regionalization on the basis of his empirical findings and theoretical understanding. When one talks of 'regional history' one attributes historical continuity and homogeneity (political, economic, cultural, etc.) and one delineates boundaries which are not necessarily congruent with the 'given' boundaries one started with.

Thus, the 'region' in historiography is a construct historians make and employ. (I prefer the term 'constructed' region to 'denoted' region.) Likewise, the linguist may construct regions: G.A. Grierson's[2] linguistic survey of India (1903–27) is a famous example. The cultural anthropologist may construct regions: the Anthropological Survey of India under Nirmal Kumar Bose[3] produced an excellent work of this kind, sadly neglected by historians. In terms of homogeneity of social structures, Satish Saberwal suggested that sociologists might regionalize with profit for it contextualizes local studies and pushes ahead beyond the level of mere sociography.

In the task of 'constructing' a region the historian, consciously or unconsciously, confronts a basic problem of homogeneity within his 'region' which is never absolute, and there are also discontinuities over time. Therefore, regionalization always brings in its wake the problem of uneven homogeneity and hazy regional boundaries. An excellent example is provided by Christopher Baker in his study of the Tamil Nadu agrarian economy, 1880–1955.[4] Baker's study reveals that the boundaries of subregions are fuzzy (and they do not, of course, correspond to the boundaries of districts which happen to be the units used in the aggregative data sources). One may get around this problem, as Subbarao suggested, by using not so much linear boundaries as the 'foci of various zones'. Economic historians and geographers also use the concept of 'nodal' region where the spatial organization of economic activity allows them to map the cultural focal place and areas around it, dependent as well as subordinate. The concept of 'nodal' region may be extended to politics where there exist focal places in a super-ordinate position over subordinate areas. In the margin the boundaries of a region (e.g. Vanga, Bangala and Bengal) may be hazy and shifting from time to time: the focal may be characterized by greater homogeneity and temporal continuity.

Regionalization in history involves hierarchization of spatial units. On the one hand, the notion of region implies a relationship to a greater whole (it may be a civilization, a nation, an empire, or an economic system, etc.), on the other hand the notion of region subsumes that of subregions. Thus, regional history chooses to concentrate at a particular level within a hierarchy of units. The tendency to neglect to relate the region to the larger unit is a crucial mistake. This point needs to be emphasized because at times there is a tendency to look at regional history in isolation. Allow me, as a student of economic history, to illustrate this point. At a time when scholars in India and abroad are expanding the framework of interpretation to situate the colonial economy of India in the context of the world system of capitalism, a meaningful analysis of regions in India is unlikely unless the analysis also comprehends in its scope the relationship between region and the colonial economic system as a whole and the world system into which it is integrated.

I have underlined the precautions that should be observed in regionalizing in history. At the same time, regional level study promises to enrich historiography in ways not achievable using the macro-level approach. In economic history this is the only way one can test generalizations of a high order, say about de-industrialization, differentiation within the peasantry, and peasant rationality in crop choice. Regional history is the appropriate level because at the all-India level many basic data are not available. Any one who has dealt with the nineteenth century statistical sources would have realized how difficult it is to construct a continuous time series on an all-India scale. Such an exercise is more feasible for some regions. Moreover, regional history allows one to explore details of the interplay between economic, social and cultural factors in the explication of some questions: How is the dominance of the rich peasant related to caste dominance? What accounts for the failure of technological innovations to catch on? How is power in rural society an instrument to keep the poor in their place? What are the forms of resistance of the exploited? There are details at the micro-level that are needed to explain big things; the large maps of a national scale cannot accommodate such details. Finally, the need to study 'history from below', the history of the historyless common man, demands that one addresses regional, or what may be called micro-level history.

These, therefore, are the rich potentials of regional history, provided one is conscious and cautious of the methodological problems. Above all, if I may repeat myself, historians must guard against the perversion of their scholarly effort in the direction of 'regionalism'. Recently, I read the first Presidential Address at the Indian History Congress (1935).[5] Sir Shafaat Ahmed Khan said, 'I dread the prospect of long lines of histories of India written by Muslims, Mahrattas, Sikhs, Bengalis and Pathans, each from their own point of view. . . . Should history be tied to the chariot wheels of perverted sectionalism which . . . is now acting as a most serious obstacle to the growing nationalism of India as a whole?'

When Sir Shafaat Ahmed Khan wrote this, he obviously did not mean to dismiss regional history but what he had in mind was a balance between the regional and the national, between the part and the whole as he conceived it.

How a region is constructed by historians is illustrated by developments in historiography in Bengal in the early decades of the twentieth century. Beyond the creation of the 'Bengal Presidency' and the 'Subah Bengal', there was a time when Rarha, Vanga and Varendra were, in common perception, separate regions. How did the Bengal intelligentsia view this separateness? Suniti Kumar Chatterjee[6] in his multivolume work argued for 'the evolution of a common nationality and of one type of culture and literature among the people of heterogeneous origins in West Bengal (Rarha), in East Bengal (Vanga), in North Bengal (Varendra)'. This, according to him, happened by the middle of tenth century AD. Around the same time, Ramaprasad Chanda's[7] work on the ruling dynasties in Bengal during the pre-Muslim period, Akshay Kumar Maitreya's[8] epigraphic research, and Rakhaldas Banerji's[9] work laid the historical foundation for the rising sentiment of regional patriotism. This sentiment was not necessarily in contradiction with an all-national loyalty, but certainly distinct from it; likewise, this regional patriotism gave a tone to the new histories of Bengal which was distinct from the tone apparent in the historical works on Bengal by Englishmen in the preceding decades. The institutional base of this new approach to the past of Bengal was in the Bangiya Sahitya Parishad or the Varendra Research Society (founded by Maitreya in 1910), not in the Englishmen's institutions like the Asiatic Society. There was also a significant change in language: the preferred medium for Maitreya, Chanda or Banerji was Bengali, not English; they virtually founded historiography in the vernacular language.

Thus, a regional identity consciousness provided the impetus to the intellectuals to reconstruct the history of their region in the first two decades of the twentieth century in Bengal. Analogous developments may be seen in other parts of India at different points of time.

An important question that has engaged the attention of many historians is the role of history in promoting identity consciousness. Those who have been happy with the development of regional identities have, on the other hand, lamented the emergence of local identities leading to further fragmentation. An apposite example is the emergence of ethnic identity consciousness in north-east India. At first it took the form of assertion of separateness in cultural terms; this consciousness also took the form of an inimical stance against neighbouring peoples. It is undeniable that some of the latter entered the north-eastern provinces of British India in a sort of sub-colonial role. Thus, an attitude of friendliness could not be expected of the indigenous population. As an indigenous educated middle class emerged, there developed a critical stance *vis-à-vis* the immigrants from neighbouring parts beyond the borders of the north-eastern provinces. In the long run, however, the feeling of 'separateness' *vis-à-vis* 'outsiders' nurtured under these circumstances seems to have engendered the feeling of 'separateness' in *indigenous* ethnic groups as well at an incremental rate. One is now witnessing some of the consequences of this progressive ethnic fermentation. Historical construction to legitimize the identity formation process at the regional or provincial level, and then at the localized ethnic levels can be traced in this historiography. Apart from the north-eastern states of Bengal, there has been a major historiographic shift—the engagement of the historian in the task of legitimizing the communal division that eventually took the form of the partition of Bengal in 1947. Here, again, the separateness of the Muslim community in Bengal, as interpreted historically, gave rise to the reinterpretation of the *Bengali* character of their culture as the dominant trend overriding the *Muslim* character of that culture.

Consider, for example, the three-volume *History of Bangladesh 1704–1971*[10] published by the Asiatic Society of Bangladesh. According to the head of the editorial board of this massive work, A.R. Mallick, 'the emergence of Bangladesh as a nation state' contributed to 'a strong feeling among scholars and general readers that the history of Bengal ought to be rewritten'. It is interesting that this rewriting of history begins from the foundation of the Nawabi rule to that of the government of Bangladesh. History, of course, is continually rewritten. But rewriting history acquires a new significance beyond the usual incremental process that routinely brings about historiographic revision. Rewriting of history as a conscious agenda of action of a new nation-state suggests a paradigmatic shift—not only elevating the 'regional' to the 'national' plane, but also reorienting the interpretation of history of a period pre-dating the factors leading to the formation of a new nation-state by decades, indeed by a century or two. These three volumes reinterpreting the former region of East Bengal or East Pakistan, now Bangladesh, do not present one single pattern of interpretation, but the common agenda of all Bangladeshi scholars represented here is to underline the separateness of Bengali identity, or at least Bengali Muslim identity. One of the editors of these volumes states:

> Never in history India was a single state or a nation. . . . In the maze of differences Bengal stood out pre-eminently from the rest of India, and, allowed uninterrupted political development, it had perhaps the brightest prospect of growing into a nation state. . . . (The British government and) distorted political developments led leaders to advance their political ideas either in terms of *akhand* Indian nationalism or two-nation theory based on religion and sectarianism. . . .[11]

For the present, the task is not to evaluate the validity of these generalizations. The concern here is with the representation of a regional/sub-national/national identity in such reinterpretation in the wake of the formation of Bangladesh, an example of the reflection of cultural and political identity formation in historiography.

The point is to underline the fact that the Muse of history, unlike the legendary Trishanku, does not float somewhere above the earth. Clio is earthbound and many would like her to be a 'daughter of the soil', if such a phrase can be used. Awareness of the consequent *representations of the past* should be part of the historians' consciousness. If my endeavour to put together some thoughts on regionalization in historiography helps to promote such awareness, my purpose will be served.

In conclusion, I would like to reiterate the point made by Sir Shafaat Ahmed Khan against regional history in an isolationist perspective. Such a narrow perspective the best of the regional historians will also eschew. I recall what Akshay Kumar Maitreya said in 1921: 'The history of the Bengali people cannot be comprehended if one limits oneself to the chronicle of what happened within the boundaries of Bengal in an isolated manner. What has been the history of Bengal is also an aspect of the history of mankind.'[12] That applies with equal force to the history of any region.

NOTES

1. J.E. Schwartzberg, 'The Evolution of Regional Power Configurations in the Indian Sub-continent', in R.G. Fox, ed., *Realm and Region in Traditional India*, Durhan: Duke, 1967, pp. 197–233.
2. G.A. Grierson, *Linguistic Survey of India*, vols. I–XI, New Delhi: Motilal Banarasidass, rpt., 1966–8.
3. Nirmal Kumar Bose, 'Cultural Zones in India', *Geographical Review of India*, vol. 18, no. 4, December 1956.
4. Christopher John Baker, *An Indian Rural Economy: The Tamilnad Countryside, 1880–1955*, New Delhi: Oxford University Press, 1984.
5. The Indian History Congress met for the first time in 1935 in Pune under the chairmanship of Sir Shafaat Ahmed Khan. It was originally known as the Modern History Congress. See Sir Shafaat Ahmed Khan, 'Presidential Address, All-India Modern History Congress', Pune, 1935, in Sabyasachi Bhattacharya, ed., *Essays in Modern Indian Economic History: Selected Essays from Indian History Congress Proceedings 1935–85*, New Delhi: Munshiram Manoharlal, 1987. See editor's 'Introduction', pp. xvi–xvii.
6. Suniti Kumar Chatterjee, *Origion and Development of the Bengali Language*, vol. 1, Calcutta: Calcutta University, 1926, p. 147.
7. Ramaprasad Chanda, *Gaur Rajamala*, Rajshahi: Barendra Research Society, 1912.
8. Akshay Kumar Maitreya, *Gaur Lekha Mala*, Rajshahi: Barendra Research Society, 1912.
9. Rakhaldas Banerji, *History of Bengal*, Calcutta: Calcutta University, 1915.
10. Sirajul Islam, ed., *History of Bangladesh, 1704–1971*, Dhaka: Asiatic Society of Bangladesh, 1992.
11. Sirajul Islam, *History of Bangladesh*, vol. 1, Chap. 15.
12. Maitreya, 'Preface', in Ramaprasad Chanda, *Gaur Rajamala*, Rajshahi: Barendra Research Society, 1912.

The Local, the Regional and the National: The Dynamics of History

Surendra Gopal

If history has logic, it is tortuous and has so far evaded comprehension, hence, a number of philosophies of history. Mention may be made of some of them: those propounded by Hegel, Marx, Toynbee and recently by Fukuyama of 'the end of history' theme. All of them attempt to cover the entire gamut of history and in the process the diverse experiences of the several groups of people in various parts of the world are glossed over. While scientific rigour beckons one to find a common cause to explain all human experiences, 'the subject matter of history', scientific honesty also demands that variations in experiences ought to be recognized, recorded and accounted for. The general and the particular are woven together to form the rich tapestry of history. The local, the regional and the national continue to interact with each other and provide the stimulus for the march of history.

Local and regional histories (the former imperceptibly merges into the latter, without, of course, losing its autonomy) assume importance if one remembers that the socialization process of human beings begins in the local context. The child's first encounter with language, solid food, dress, norms of behaviour, life-style, etc., are all local. The local is firmly etched in his memory and psychology. Local histories are an inescapable part of the discipline. It may be noted that local and regional histories cannot *ipso facto* provide instant building blocks for national history; they interact but each has its autonomy. Nevertheless, they remain an integral part of national history.

Let me illustrate this with reference to two peasant protest movements which took place in Mithila and Champaran, situated respectively, in the north-east and north-west parts of the modern state of Bihar. They belong to two different cultural zones, though being a mere speck on the map of India. Both have in their own ways enriched and influenced national history.

From the late eighteenth and the beginning of the nineteenth century, Europeans began to participate in the indigo trade in Bihar: first, as exporters of the dye to England. As time progressed, they took to manufacturing. Since the profits were enormous, by the second half of the nineteenth century they turned to cultivation of indigo as well. European monopoly in indigo was a consequence of the English conquest of Bihar and Bengal at the battles of Plassey (1757) and Buxar (1764). The political servitude of Bihar and Bengal ushered in far-reaching changes in the local economy by forcibly promoting indigo cultivation in place of cereals and making it the premier crop. While Europeans had started coffee plantations in south India, tea plantations in north-east India, they concentrated on indigo plantations in Bengal and Bihar. With the passage of time, they had to leave Bengal as their activities led to strong local protests and they eventually concentrated on Bihar. The compulsion to develop Bengal and Bihar as the primary sources for the supply of indigo dye instead of traditional areas in the preceding two centuries, such as Gujarat, north-east Rajasthan (Biana indigo was supposed to be the best in India), Agra, and Lahore, can be explained in terms of the persisting demand for the commodity as well as sweeping changes in the political map of India in the eighteenth and early nineteenth centuries. The eclipse of pan Indian powers like the Mughals and the Marathas and the rise of regional states such as the Punjab, Awadh and the fragmentation of Rajasthan, made procurement of the dye in the traditional areas expensive, difficult and hazardous and rendered its transportation to the port of Surat extremely uncertain and risky.

With the increase in the number of textile factories in England as a result of the Industrial Revolution, indigo dye had a ready market. The textile manufacturers of England looked for a secure, steady and cheap supply base and this they found in India which had provided indigo since the English East India Company began its trading operations there at the beginning of the seventeenth century. The logic of the colonial economy was clear: the metropolis concentrated on manufacturing activities; the colonies provided the raw materials as well as market for the manufactured goods. The political control of Bengal and Bihar and the availability of the Calcutta port for shipping the dye to England influenced their decision to develop indigo plantations in Bihar in the second half of the nineteenth century. The local, the regional and the world system were continuously interacting with each other.

By the first half of the nineteenth century, European indigo plantations were firmly established in Bihar and Bengal. The progress of these plantations can be gauged from the fact that in 1850 there were 64 indigo concerns in north Bihar (where the beginning was made in 1782 by Francois Grand, the collector of Muzaffarpur). In Darbhanga, Europeans set up indigo factories in 1801 and three of them were at Hathauri, Pupri and Kamtaul.[1] Of these, Pandoul (situated in the estate of Darbhanga—the largest in Bihar) was the largest, covering an area of 10,500 acres, roughly 300 sq. miles. It had under its jurisdiction nine factories within a radius of 16 miles and its owner was John Gale.

It should be remembered that the growth of the Pandoul Indigo Factory coincided with the death of Maharaja Maheshwar Singh on 21 October 1860. Lakshmishwar Singh who succeeded him was an infant. The estate was taken over by the Court of Wards on 23 October 1860 under instructions from the government. James Forlong, a former European indigo planter was appointed Manager, and on 9 February 1861 he took charge from a Deputy Magistrate, originally entrusted with this office.

The local zamindar cowed down by the prestige enjoyed by European indigo planters as members of the ruling class was in no position to pay heed to the adverse consequences which flowed for the local economy from this development. The farmers were coerced to grow indigo on their best land—*bheet* or upland. Even when they were not willing to raise an indigo crop and were inclined to sow cereals, they were compelled to plant indigo by the European planters. The situation became unbearable for the farmers because of the oppressive behaviour of the planters, who forced the farmers to send their bullocks for ploughing their fields. Those who dared to refuse were dragged before the indigo planter; the tenants were confined in a *murgi khana* or cubicles built for rearing chickens. This was the ultimate humiliation for many of the farmers were upper caste Hindus and strict vegetarians. The local zamindar, Maharaja Lakshmishwar Singh of Darbhanga, being a minor was in no position to help his tenants; he could neither save their honour nor prevent their economic exploitation.

In order to understand the process of colonization of the Indian economy, it is important to study the economic policies and practices of colonial administration in Bengal and Bihar in the nineteenth century. Regional history in this context explains the genesis, origin and growth of colonial economic policies and practices which eventually contributed to the economic impoverishment of Bihar and Bengal.

The people were discontented. The vernacular press was in the process of being set up and the English language press would not air their grievances. There was no leadership among the oppressed to mobilize the discontent and to devise a strategy for redress of their grievances. The bureaucracy, supposed to ensure equitable enforcement of law, for a variety of reasons had adopted a partisan attitude toward indigo planters.

The mounting discontent was sparked off by the famine which gripped Bihar in 1866. It was not a sudden occurrence. The price of rice had been steadily increasing. In 1863, 35 seers of rice could be purchased for a rupee. In 1866, the price rose sharply and 7 seers of rice were available for a rupee. The peasants wanted to sow cereal crops which would not only be a safeguard against hunger, but also economically more profitable. But the indigo planter forbade them to do so. People's discontent turned into anger. Cutting across caste and religious lines, people united and refused to yield to the terrorist tactics used by the owner of the Pandoul Indigo Factory. The agitation broke out towards the end of 1866.

At this point it is interesting to recall that Anderson, owner of the Kamtaul Indigo Factory, acted as the General Manager of the Darbhanga Raj between 21 April and 16 November 1866. As distinguished from other European indigo planters in the region, he was seen as 'wise', 'kind' and a 'friend of the poor'. May be his refusal to back the bullying tactics of Gale, emboldened the raiyats to take a stand against Gale's unjust and exploitative economic policies. Initially, the local administration paid no heed to the storm that was brewing. But the Lt. Governor of Bengal realized the gravity of the situation and believed that the upsurge could spread beyond Pandoul, and that the events of 1857 may be re-enacted. He repeatedly instructed the local officials to force the recalcitrant owner of the Pandoul Indigo Factory to come to an understanding with the raiyats. Barbour, the Sub Divisional Magistrate, believed that the demands of the raiyats were just. He refused to be bullied by the indigo planter and stood by the raiyats. With the estate and the local bureaucracy arrayed against him, Gale realized that the state apparatus would not come to his aid. Left with no option he was forced to negotiate with the agitating raiyats; the movement—the first recorded instance of collective defiance of a European indigo planter in Bihar—came to a successful end. The raiyats extorted several concessions. Though violence was in the air till the settlement took place, things ended peacefully. The colonial state, however, did not permit Barbour to pass an order detrimental to the interest of the indigo planter. He was told, '. . . this is a matter with which . . . Government officers cannot interfere. They can keep the peace and settle questions of disputed possession and punish trespass and mischief.'[2] When it suited its economic interests, the colonial state had no reservations about invoking the *liassez-faire* policy, propounded by economist Adam Smith.

Such an agitation against indigo planters was not repeated in Pandoul, though when the freedom movement engulfed the entire country, there were several agitations especially in the 1930s.[3] By then, thanks to Gandhi's leadership in the anti-colonial struggle, the local, the regional and the national had coalesced.

The agitation was a local event which broke out because the

locals perceived the injustice of the acts of omissions and commissions of the indigo planters. But it was eventually precipitated by the hunger and hardship brought about by the famine which engulfed the province in 1866. The regional factor had acted as a catalyst for the outbreak of the local movement.

The oppression of the European indigo planter continued but the next two decades were comparatively trouble free. During this period, however, things continued to worsen in Champaran. A number of factors helped to maintain peace in Pandoul. Under the Court of Wards, the administration of the estate became efficient and its finances improved. Maharaja Lakshmishwar Singh, when he came of age, took the reins of administration in his own hands. He worked to improve the financial health of the estate and was held in great esteem for intorducing public welfare programmes. Eventually, he purchased the Pandoul Indigo Factory and the cause of friction between the planter and the local populace was eliminated.

The oppressive character of the plantation economy did not end in other parts of Bihar as it was ingrained in the nature of the colonial system. The plantation economy was an integral part of the colonial economy which appeared in the nineteenth century as a result of the expansion of European imperialism. Europeans set up sugar, tea, coffee, rubber, and indigo plantations in their colonies and earned huge profits. Where they deemed economical, slave/indentured labour was employed.

Bihar was found suitable for indigo plantation. Local conditions forbade Europeans from employing slave/indentured labour. They tried to make up the loss by using forced labour, levying extra-legal taxes and cesses and commandeering various kinds of services from the population. Local history reveals various facets of colonial exploitation, practised in different areas. It is through local histories that the multidimensional character of events influencing regional, national or even world history can be fully appreciated. The local has the potential to influence regional history (though sometimes only fleetingly), as is evident from the following example.

The success of the agitators must have been orally transmitted across the region, especially in the contiguous area to the south and west up to the borders of UP where European indigo factories were in operation. The nature of exploitation of the population of the area was almost similar; only the intensity and details varied due to the personality of the indigo planters and the psyche of the people the planters were dealing with.[4]

Champaran lying in the north-west corner of Bihar and almost due west of Pandoul had a number of indigo plantations. European indigo planters of Champaran followed the same repressive policies as their counterparts in Pandoul. The situation was aggravated by the pro-European tilt almost amounting to collaboration by the Bettiah zamindar, who was in dire financial straits and was raising loans in England. A time came when things became unbearable. The tension could not be defused because the local bureaucracy was oblivious of the suffering of the people and let things drift.

The Officiating Magistrate of Motihari wrote to the Commissioner of Patna Division that peasants belonging to the villages of Doelta, Sonowl, Subhoa, Khudda and Sugowlee had complained that they were being forced to cultivate indigo. The result was '. . . throughout the entire year we are dragged to labour day and night'. The officials informed their superiors that in certain cases the peasants had already sowed *Cheena* crops instead of indigo in defiance of the wishes of the planters. Faced with peasant obduracy, the indigo planters and the officials adopted an inflexible approach. The bureaucracy did not take any positive steps to assuage the roused feelings of the peasantry. In the ensuing confrontation, a section of the peasants resorted to violence. The Lalsaraiya factory was set on fire.[5] McLeod, the owner of Lalsaraiya Kothi, was known as 'the king of planters' because he had 120 horses in his stable. The peasants of the neighbouring village torched the bungalow of another indigo planter.[6] Troops had to be rushed in to suppress the indigo raiyats.

Earlier in Pandoul, a negotiated settlement had been reached. However, in Champaran both sides wanted to talk from a position of strength; uneasy peace descended. Half a century of confrontation between the European indigo planters and the raiyats ensued. Fights, murder, arson and institution of court cases became the order of the day. Discontent simmered for a couple of months before a semblance of normalcy was restored.

Later, the causes of this agitation were diagnosed by government officers. They pointed to the caste affinities of a section of the peasantry of Pandoul with that of Tirhut, of which Pandoul was a part. According to them, some raiyats had come down from Tirhut and had narrated the story of their success in the campaign against the European owner of the Pandoul Indigo Factory; this had enthused the local masses. Mr. Gibbon, the first English Manager of Bettiah Raj asserted, '. . . a number of Tirhoot ryots having gone into Champaran and there taken the oath to throw in their lot with the malcontents of that district and to refuse all compromises which were not acceptable to them.'[7]

The age-old oral tradition had effectively communicated the history of a local movement in Pandoul which in turn helped to stoke the fires of discontent in Champaran where the indigo raiyats were subjected to similar oppression and gave rise to another protest movement. The local was fusing into the regional.

The transition from the local to the regional, in this case, helps to pinpoint some of the undercurrents of the historical process at work. Even when the means of surface transport basically consisted of boats, bullocks, horses, palanquins and walking, oral communication was effective. Caste solidarities could not only overcome geographical distances, but also ensure community mobilization for a common cause. Second, the unfolding of the movement brings out the differences which cultural zones exercise on the psyche of the people, especially in the absence of a common leadership or a common philosophy to guide and sustain the movement.

The Champaran peasants were part of the Bhojpuri linguistic and cultural zone, traditionally known for supplying soldiers to the armed forces of the Mughals and, later the English East India Company. As recently as the uprising of 1857, Europeans had to face the wrath of the local population. Only the arrival of additional forces enabled the government to quell the rebellion. Hence, the discontent in Champaran, when it came to fore, assumed a violent form.

Furthermore, while a number of local factors contributed to placate the peasantry of Pandaul or Mithila region in the following decades, the unrest in Champaran did not die out, it continued to simmer. Violence was not eschewed, though resort to law courts was co-opted as a part of the peasant strategy to deal with the oppressive policies of the indigo planters. Local history helps to appreciate the subtle changes that take place in the on-going historical process; in this case against the colonial economic practices.

The intervention of law courts meant that the peasant had to move out of his rural milieu; he travelled to urban centres like the district court at Motihari and interacted with the English educated Indian urban elite. He had an encounter with the depersonalized colonial administration. Not finding a satisfactory response, he proceeded to Patna and finally approached the High Court at Calcutta. There was no dearth of Bhojpuri-speaking compatriots in Calcutta, many of whom did odd jobs to earn a living. With the introduction of railways, the time and the travails of a 700-mile long journey were reduced. This gave the Champaran peasant an opportunity to assess and appreciate the technological changes that not only crucially affected him, but were sweeping across the country as well. This broadened his mental horizon, and also introduced an additional factor in his ongoing movement. His story, either by word of mouth or through occasional press coverage, became known to a wider audience, both Indian and non-Indian, government functionaries and non-officials, educated and uneducated.

The protest of the indigo peasants of Champaran became a part of the struggle of the indigo peasants of Bengal as well. It was viewed in a broader perspective after the indigo revolt of Pabna (in East Bengal) in 1871. The local movement of Pandoul indirectly helped to put the problems of indigo farmers on the national agenda through the agency of the peasants of Champaran. But nearly four decades elapsed before the problem hit the nation in the face.

The relentless struggle of the raiyats of Champaran against the indigo planters assumed a variety of forms; they appealed to the higher administrative functionaries; they took recourse to individual and group defiance of the indigo planters and their hirelings; they instituted court cases against the planters and even appealed to the High Court in Calcutta. Once in a while, they also used arms.

The prolonged struggle of the Champaran peasantry attracted some media attention since it refused to be either cowed down or pacified in spite of repression and occasional sops offered by the planters and the government. The continuing struggle obliterated the boundaries of caste, class and religion. Upper and lower castes among the Hindus and Muslims and tribals, all united to raise their voice in protest. The colonial administration remained largely unmoved since in the first decade of the twentieth century there was a breakdown of authority and the outbreak of large-scale violence.

The continuity of the movement coincided with an increase in the number of participants—a definite sign that it was taking deep roots among all sections of society. The leadership for the movement was provided by semi-literate and illiterate peasants. It was for this reason that the colonial administration and the indigo planters largely ignored it and were unable to fathom the intensity of disaffection. Local history reveals the causes, contents and course of the movement. In the process, it illustrates how national events start impinging upon the local and impart to it new import and meanings.

A proximate cause of peasant unrest was gross financial mismanagement of the Bettiah Raj under which were the lands of the peasants. It paid no heed to the problems faced by the peasantry. As the Bettiah estate depended on the indigo planters for financial assistance, the latter had a stranglehold on the administration of the estate. An indigo planter by the name of Gibbon[8] became the Manager, and the peasants had to directly deal with the European indigo planters, who became increasingly arbitrary in their behaviour towards the raiyats.

The zamindars of the Bettiah Raj failed to protect the tenants *vis-à-vis* the European indigo planters, a crucial difference between the tenants of Pandoul and those of Champaran. While the condition of the Champaran raiyats worsened, Indian society witnessed a number of changes which had an impact on Bihar as well. The formation of the Indian National Congress in 1885 had brought together educated Indians on one platform; originally they were concerned with greater representation in the higher echelons of the bureaucracy. Gradually, they began to focus on the plight of their poor and uneducated brethren who suffered because of the discriminatory policies of the colonial government. When prayers and petitions did not suffice, some educated Indians resorted to bombs. The bomb hurled by Khudiram Bose and Prafulla Chaki in Muzaffarpur on 30 April 1908 opened the eyes of the common man to the fact that his discontent was shared by Indians in other regions as well. Second, the role of the English and the vernacular press was growing. The latter, particularly, took up the cause of the oppressed masses in the countryside. A considerable section of the readership of the vernacular press included semi-literates, both urban and rural. Since literacy rates were low, barely 2 per cent, much information was circulated by word of mouth. Rural India, including the backwaters of Champaran, was no longer unaware of what was going on in the world and in other parts of India.

Finally, members of religious movements such as the Brahmo Samaj and the Arya Samaj which had emerged in the nineteenth century travelled all over the country, preaching the message of their organization both through printed word and lectures. They were trying to work after the manner of Christian missionaries. The Arya Samaj founded in 1875 in Bombay by Swami Dayanand had targeted north India. Its *pracharaks* or preachers had reached Champaran. While talking of preserving Hinduism and purging it of accretions like the caste system, untouchability and other social evils, they also spoke of freedom and overthrowing the British as the panacea for many economic ills.

The Champaran peasantry, almost wholly illiterate, was convinced by these preachers of the righteousness of their cause. They were filled with deep indignation and the long struggle only made them more determined and bold against their oppressors. It did not come as a surprise when Bloomfield, Manager of Telahara Kothi (already notorious for his moral lapses), was killed while on a tour for misbehaving with a village woman.[9] This incident set in motion a fresh wave of peasant agitation in 1907. Many future peasant leaders such as Raj Kumar Shukla, Sheikh Gulab and Sheetal Rai emerged during this period. They were imprisoned; they appealed against their conviction and were finally acquitted by the Calcutta High Court.[10] The four decades during which the Champaran peasants kept alive their movement saw developments in the national arena which helped to sustain the morale of the people of Champaran. They emerged more determined to fight for their cause.

The interaction of the local, regional and national explains the dynamics of history. Of course, at the same time, each of three components has its own autonomy. When and how that autonomy is exercised, cannot be explained at this moment. A decade later, in 1917, the local, the regional and the national interacted once again in Champaran. This time the outcome gave a new direction to the history of India.

From hindsight it appears that this was possible because Raj Kumar Shukla and Pir Muhammad Moonis became close friends. Raj Kumar Shukla was a moderately well-off farmer, semi-literate and had at one time served as a clerk in the Bettiah Raj. He had also looked after the landed property of a brahman landholder who spent most of his time in Allahabad. He had resisted the tyranny of the indigo planters and had participated in the movement of 1907–8, for which he had been gaoled. He was determined to secure justice for the raiyats and was willing to fight tooth and nail the system which had caused so much humiliation and economic misery to the local population. He had instituted cases in law courts and was in contact with lawyers like Braj Kishore Prasad and Rajendra Prasad, who were important members of the Indian National Congress and were sympathetic to the cause of the peasantry. Pir Muhammad Moonis had served as a teacher in a school run by the Bettiah Raj but had been dismissed for espousing the cause of the raiyats. He persisted in his campaign and wrote in the vernacular press on the issue. Moonis, a freelance journalist, and Raj Kumar Shukla, a farmer, were bound by a common cause and proved a perfect foil for each other. A Muslim and a Hindu were united in their hatred against the tyranny of the European indigo planters. It is possible that Moonis must have informed Shukla of the Congress as a forum to garner support for the cause of the peasantry. Also, the lawyers with whom Shukla was in contact must have concurred with this view. The role of the Congress and its leaders appeared to be effective in the eyes of both these men to redress their grievances against the European indigo planters.

Undoubtedly, this perception must have prompted Moonis and Shukla to attend the provincial session of the Indian National Congress held at Chapra on 3 April 1915 and to describe the plight of the raiyats to the delegates. The issue of indigo raiyats in Champaran had been placed before the people of Bihar by the victims themselves and therefore no further authentication was needed. Encouraged by the positive response, they decided to raise the issue before a national audience at the annual session of the Indian National Congress which was convened at Lucknow in December 1916. This was Champaran's tryst with destiny; the local was soon to became a part of the national.

Within a year, Moonis and Shukla's outlook underwent a complete transformation. For them, the salvation of Champaran lay in the support they could garner at the national level. For them, the basic issue in Champaran was human dignity—it transcended political, economic and social grievances. All energies and efforts were directed towards righting the grievous wrong perpetrated by the indigo planters. All along, the local was subsumed by the regional. It had taken half a century of continued struggle to put Champaran on the provincial political agenda and to involve local political activists like Braj Kishore Prasad in this struggle. They were prepared to discuss the issue at a national forum where fellow Indians from different parts of the country had gathered and were willing to listen to a simple peasant expressing his concern about the oppressive measures used by the indigo planters. From then onwards Champaran was included in the national agenda.

At the Lucknow session of the Indian National Congress in December 1916, Braj Kishore Prasad introduced a resolution on

Champaran which was seconded by Raj Kumar Shukla. Though the resolution was passed, Shukla knew from experience that pious words did not mean anything to the European indigo planters. A struggle had to be waged both against the indigo planters and the colonial regime. Local issues merely reflected the surface tension of the colonial policy which, despite its commitment to the rule of law, in actual practice, favoured the Europeans, the bureaucracy and those who could manipulate the law. Shukla and Moonis had for the first time clearly and correctly identified the real enemies of the raiyats, the indigo planters and the bureaucracy. By themselves they were no match for these powerful adversaries. Hence, they decided that the leadership for the impending struggle must be provided by one familiar with the nuances of the power structure which sustained the authoritarian colonial regime. Moreover, the new leader should be totally committed to the cause of the raiyats. No local political leader of the requisite stature could be found in Champaran. Despite their support to the cause of the rural poor, regional leaders had never participated in any peasant struggle nor had they led any mass movement. Leadership, therefore, had to come from outside Bihar and they knew that it was their duty to find it, since they were the victims. Faced with this dilemma, Shukla and Moonis decided to approach national leaders assembled at Lucknow such as Madan Mohan Malaviya and Bal Gangadhar Tilak. However, none of these leaders were inclined to offer any help because of their unfamiliarity with the situation in Champaran and inability to see how could it become a part of the national agenda. At this point they were advised to approach Gandhi, who had returned to India in 1915 after successfully challenging the apartheid policy in South Africa. Since they were familiar with Gandhi's name and fame, they decided to meet him and request him to lead their struggle. The two activists from Bihar had no hesitation in approaching a non-Bihari, who did not understand their language and who had no prior knowledge of their problems. The only thing in his favour was that he had experience of guiding and leading a mass struggle against the colonial rulers, though in a foreign country. Gandhi had no idea where Champaran was and what was the nature of problem for which these men had sought to enlist his support. Initially he refused, but he soon revised his decision because of the dogged persistence of Raj Kumar Shukla, who continued to meet him even after the session had ended. He promised to visit Champaran on his tour of Calcutta in a few months' time. How can one explain the trust reposed in Gandhi by Raj Kumar Shukla and Moonis? Obviously, they were imbued by a feeling of pan-Indian nationalism, which prompted them to rise above local and regional considerations. It was also a triumph of the rising tide of Indian nationalism, which had penetrated to remote areas like Champaran and had influenced the thinking of semi-literate people. Raj Kumar Shukla displayed his tenacity and dedication to the cause of the raiyats. The moment Gandhi informed him of his arrival in Calcutta, he rushed to Calcutta. Having no idea of Gandhi's address in Calcutta he barged into a newspaper office and got the address. Shukla persuaded Gandhi to accompany him to Champaran. History was being made. Moved by Shukla's earnestness, a leader of international stature decided to take up a local issue and throw behind it his expertise in leading mass agitations.

When Gandhi arrived in Champaran in April 1917, the colonial administration and the European indigo planters immediately realized the gravity of the situation. They were aware that Gandhi would act as a rallying point for the long suppressed peasantry, desperately looking for a saviour. Educated Biharis with a social conscience rushed to Champaran to help Gandhi, since he was neither familiar with the local language nor with the situation obtaining in Champaran. The local had suddenly become a regional and national concern. The bureaucracy tried to prevent Gandhi from conducting inquiries. A government order asked him to leave the district. When he refused, a case was instituted against him. He put up a resolute legal defence. This fact underscored that the writ of law should run countrywide notwithstanding the whims and fancies of the local officials. The treatment meted out to Gandhi aroused the nation's concern. The Governor of Bihar was forced to intervene. The restrictions imposed on him were withdrawn. The people were relieved of their fears and anxieties. They recorded their grievances, spoke about the injustice and indignities heaped on them and signed their statements. The European indigo planters also had their say but the statements of the peasants carried greater conviction. The attention of the entire nation was focused on Gandhi and Champaran. Public leaders all over the country talked of Gandhi's successful non-violent intervention and the national press published stories of the sea change in Champaran. Champaran had suddenly become a matter of national concern.

The government and the Governor of Bihar conceded the demands of the peasantry. A committee of enquiry was set up on 12 June 1917 to inquire into 'the relations between landlord and tenant in Champaran district' and also 'into all disputes arising out of the manufacture and cultivation of indigo'.[11]

This was Gandhi's first encounter with rural India. It was also his maiden brush with the Indian colonial machinery. His success in forcing the colonial regime to accept the genuine demands of the peasantry without mounting an agitation transformed the Indian political scene. It was clear that Gandhi's strategy which was successful in a micro-region in mitigating the condition of the oppressed could be applied to solve the greatest problem facing the country—freedom from the colonial yoke. Half a century of continued agitation and a combination of fortuitous circumstances had catapulted Champaran into the forefront of the national agenda. The local defined the parameters of the national discourse.

It was truly national because in Champaran Gandhi came face to face with abject poverty, near total illiteracy and suppression of women. They called for immediate reforms and Gandhi was quick to respond. He summoned his fellow workers from Maharashtra and Gujarat, his wife Kasturba and son Devadas, to work in the villages of Champaran. It was obvious that the struggle for political independence, social reform and economic development must be launched simultaneoulsy throughout the country. This was the lesson Champaran taught the country. More than this, the Congress leadership realized that it had to go to the masses. Annual conferences and well-drafted resolutions would not move the colonial masters. Only a mass upsurge would force the alien rulers to grant political independence. Mass mobilization under Gandhi became an irrevocable part of the Congress agenda. Barely three years later, Gandhi launched the nation-wide non-cooperation movement. The local, the regional and the national had fused together. Such examples are not hard to find if one examines the history of other areas as well.

NOTES

1. Hetukar Jha, ed., *A Glimpse of Tirhut in the Second Half of the Nineteenth Century: Riaz-i-Tirhut of Ayodhya Prasad 'Bahar'*, Kameshwar Singh Bihar Heritage Series, 3, Darbhana: Maharajadhiraja Kameshwar Singh Kalyani Foundation, 1997, p. 52.
2. Letter no. 48 dated 7 February 1867, Patna Commissioner to the Secretary to the Government of Bengal, Patna Commissioner Record Series, vol. I, Basta V.
3. See Wendy Singer, *Creating Histories*, New Delhi: Oxford University Press, 1997, Chaps. VIII, XIX.
4. Ayodhya Prasad 'Bahar', the author of *Riaz-i-Tirhut*, speaks glowingly of the character of Mr. Anderson, the owner of Kamtaul Indigo Factory–one of the first three indigo factories established in the Darbhanga region in 1801. He describes him as 'sober, wise and kind; a father-figure to the *raiyats*, and a friend to the poor; god-fearing, without arrogance; always smiling and soft-spoken . . .', op. cit., p. 52.
5. C.E. Buckland, *Bengal under the Lieutenant Governors*, vol. I, Calcutta: S.K. Lahiri and Co., 1901, pp. 430–1.
6. G. Mishra, *The Agrarian Problems of Permanent Settlement: A Case study of Champaran*, New Delhi: People's Publishing House, 1978, p. 236.
7. Patna Commissioner's Record Series, vol. 1, Basta 6, Letter no. 2, Confidential from Officiating Collector of Tirhoot to Commissioner, Revenue, Patna, 9 April 1968.

8. Girish Mishra, *The Agrarian Problems*, op. cit., p. 38.
9. B.B. Mishra, ed., *Select Documents on Mahatma Gandhi's Movement in Champaran, 1917–19*, Patna: Government of Bihar, 1963, p. 15.
10. S.K. Mittal, *Peasant Uprisings and Mahatma Gandhi in North Bihar*, Meerut: Ann Prakashan, 1978, p. 101.
11. M. Razi Ahmad, *Indian Peasant Movement and Mahatma Gandhi*, New Delhi: Shabd Prakashan, 1987, p. 173.

Varna Ratnakara and its Ethnography

K.S. Singh

I will discuss the ethnographic dimensions of *Varna Ratnakara* (hereafter referred to as *VR*) a fourteenth century classic work edited by Suniti Kumar Chatterjee and Babua Mishra, published in 1940. The Asiatic Society of Bengal has been requested by the highest literary body of the country to bring out a re-issue in recognition of the literary and historical value of this Maithili classic.

Over the last 20 years, I have examined Kavishekharacharya Jyotirishwara Thakur's masterpiece a number of times as I have tried to explore the historical ethnography of the country. This work has enhanced my understanding of the endogenous processes of identification, formation, listing, ranking and relationship of various *jatis* and varnas. I have read *VR* in the original and relied on my rudimentary knowledge of Maithili for gaining an understanding of it.

Kavishekharacharya Jyotirishwara Thakur was deeply involved in the life and activities of his period. He wrote two books, *Dhurta Samagam* and *Panchashayak*. The latter was on the lines of Vatsyayana's *Kamasutra*, describing, among other things, the characteristics of women in different parts of the country. The influence of eroticism is also evident in *VR*. He had a zest for life and possessed a holistic view of life which was shaped by life affirmative principles of the traditions of Mithila, its philosophy of Nyaya and its *karmakanda*, its tradition of *shakti* worship and *tantra*. He was a Vedic priest and a linguist.

Chatterjee describes *VR* as the oldest work in prose in Maithili literature, a window on life at the court, which was in 'intimate touch with the commonalty', a 'valuable commentary on the epigraphic and other literary records of the contemporary and earlier period'. It is an 'all-embracing compendium of life and culture in medieval India' based on information collected from textual sources in Sanskrit and from a lifetime observation of Mithila. The author claims that he was an observer and a participant. He deftly uses the Maithili word *dekhu* or 'observe' in this connection. This work can also be seen as one of the many works of compendia (or *ratnakara*) written about the same time, according to Chatterjee. Its format is suggestive. It is divided into eight chapters called *kallol* or waves or streams which merge into the ocean or *ratnakara*. Set in the first quarter of the fourteenth century, this work was composed in the capital of a kingdom which was relatively independent. The author describes life at the court, the market and the processes of urbanization, he is equally familiar with rural life as evident from the description of *jatis*.

The author has used the term varna for the title of the book. Varna has been used in more sense than one. It is meant to be a description or an order or a schema or arrangement. Varna has also been used to denote colour. In Vidyapati, slaves of different skin colours fetched different prices. Varna has been used in this work in terms not only of social classes or *jatis*, but also in terms of ecological and cultural categories, which is understandable in a compendium like this. Thus, there are descriptions of various rivers, oceans, pilgrim centres, days and nights, seasons and so on juxtaposed with the textual material on various types of instruments, music, dress and ornaments, puranas, etc. In early literature, varna rather than *jati* was used more frequently. In later literature, varna has been used extensively for *jati*; still later varna and *jati* have been used interchangeably. In popular parlance *jati* has been used more often in parts of eastern India for all categories of communities including Muslims and linguistic groups.

However, a shortcoming of the text of the work available today is that it is incomplete; 17 out of 77 folios are missing including one to nine folios which in all probability dealt with the locale of the work, the nation of Bharat or Mithila and quite a number of communities of *mand jati* category as also others. Therefore, one can only speculate on these missing links. At one level, this work can be seen as the epitome of the identity of Mithila and its people. In current literature, identity is an all-embracing concept defined by territory, language, dress and ornaments, cuisine and other indicators. As the first few pages are missing, one can only speculate on the author's probable description of Bharat and Mithila. Bharat as a term has been in use from a very early period, and was also used in medieval literature. Shankar Deo of Assam who travelled to Puri and visited Kabir's *mazzar* at Magakar saluted Bharat in one of his compositions. *VR*, as will be discussed later, has an all-India perspective. In its earlier incarnation Mithila was Vaishali Vaideh, which had emerged as a large, distinct politico-cultural region very early in history. During the early Gupta period, Videha and Vaishali merged to form the new and larger administrative and political unit of Tirabhukti (AD 329) or Tirhut, as it came to be known later for the whole of north Bihar. Tirhut is also mentioned in medieval Persian sources. References to Mithila in vernacular literature generally described it as a cultural region lying south of the Himalayas encompassing the *terai* of Nepal and the plains of north Bihar bounded by the river Gandak on the west and the river Kosi on the east which consituted the boundary with Bengal. The present Mithila converges on the four linguistic–cultural regions of Angika. Vajjika, Bhojpuri and Magahi.

The fourteenth century witnessed the flowering of Maithili language, *VR* being one of the earliest works in the language. The following century, the age of Vidyapati, was described as the golden period of Maithili which influenced the literary traditions in Bengal. Mithila lay across the routes to Bengal and therefore a part of it, Darbhanga was known as the doorway to north Bengal (Dwara Banga). The etymology of Darbhanga, the earliest reference to which is traced to the twelfth century AD is also said to have been derived from two words *daru* and *bhanga,* i.e. the felling of trees, as the jungle was cleared, and the area was settled or the capital established. It is interesting to note that there is a tract of 40 villages peopled by the Mundas called Dalbhanga (i.e. breaking two) in Ranchi/Singhbhum districts. The Mundas circulated the twigs (*dal*) of the Sal tree held sacred by them in times of revolt as a token of invitation to their people to join in the battle against aliens. One does not know if there is any connection between this Austric word and Darbhanga, but if *VR* is any evidence, Mithila was lush green, with a rich variety of fauna and flora which, if they had survived, would have been an environmentalist's delight. Migration of communities from upper India to Assam occurred along these routes. The armies, too, moved along these routes from Delhi or Jaunpur to Lukhanauti and yet it is surprising that Mithila could safeguard its independence for a very long time until it was annexed by the Delhi Sultanate in AD 1324. Similarly, *VR* mentions the identity indicators of Mithila in terms of dress (pag) or food (rice-curd and sweets) which is consumed by all sections of people. At another level, *VR* could also be seen as Mithila's perspective on the rest of the country called Bharat or Hindustan in medieval literature. In fact, *VR* is a combination of not only a regional listing of communities and categories, but also of a national or countrywide listing of communities and categories. This feature was brought home to me as I compared the listing of communities given in this work with similar listings available elsewhere. The *Arthashastra, the Manusamhita* and the *Mahabharat* provide pan-Indian lists of communities. To these works, may be added Abul Fazl's *Ain-i-Akbari* which provides a complete list of dominant lineages belonging to all castes and creeds in Akbar's empire. *VR* contains a list of communities not only of Mithila, but also of a large part of the country. In fact, it lists 201 communities (see Appendix). *VR* also reproduces the Sanskrit notion or terms of regions and territories (*sthana* and *desh*) such as Chola, Chauhan (?), Gaum (Gaur), Malava, Gujrat, Maharashtra, Vahal (Multan) and Sinhal; a few are unintelligible, Daahal, Marar, Khorasan Netal and Bot (Tibet) have been added. *VR* does not mention the cultural change in and political transformation of these regions in the medieval period. Gandhar was no longer a part of India. It also reproduces the textual list of rivers: Ganga, Yamuna, Narmada, Saraswati, Tamraparni, Gomati, Vitasta, Kaushki, Vagvati, Kaveri, etc. It identifies pilgrim centres all over India up to Setubandh and Gangasagar. These lists of rivers and pilgrim centres constitute the fourteenth century perspective on the Hindu universe extending beyond the geographical limits of Mithila. The *Ain-i-Akbari* also provides a similar picture of the world of Hindu religion extending beyond the limits of Akbar's empire, as revealed by the description of pilgrim centres of the south.

However, *VR* is also Mithila-specific and in this sense its listing of communities can be compared with the regional listing of communities available in different parts of India either in textual material or in inscriptions including temple inscriptions. These two perspectives, Mithila-specific and the pan-Indian one, should be kept in mind while analysing the lists of *jatis* contained in *VR*. The author mentions two distinct categories, *mand* and *bhadra*, but the various *jatis* listed by him can be classified into as many as eight categories (see Appendix). The first is the category of *mand jati* under which he includes 40 *jatis*. As already discussed, this list is obviously incomplete because a few of the earlier folios are missing. The notion of *mand jatis* can be compared with that of *hin jatis* mentioned in early Sanskrit literature. An analysis of the *jatis* suggests that it is a heterogeneous category consisting of *jatis* of various statuses. Many *jatis* including 'service castes' in *VR* have been identified with present-day *jatis* or their segments: Tongar with Gongal, Dhaol with Dhaul, Dhangal with Dhangar, Bhal with Bhar, Dhalikar with Dharkar (basket maker), etc. It is interesting to note that the extent of equivalence of *mand jatis* with present-day *jatis* or their segments has been highest, compared with that of other categories mentioned in *VR*.

The next category is that of *bhadra jatis* which brings to mind the notion of *bhadralok* prevalent in adjacent Bengal. Many *jatis* under this category are evidently missing. For example, the brahmans with their five subcastes and a large number of *mool* (sept); the Karna Kayastha groups are also missing. The Cheros who had emerged as a dominant ruling lineage in western Bihar and a part of north Bihar that lay within Mithila are missing. Included in this category is the Rajputra, though *VR* mentions it separately, which again is a term that appears in contemporary

Sanskrit literature. However, Vidyapati uses the local term Rajput. *VR* lists as many as 71 Rajput clans, though the Sanskrit texts of the period mention only 36. This could be due to the proliferation of the local *jatis* of Rajputs, which emerged as ruling lineages in Mithila or in the adjoining regions. Of particular interest in this connection is the local Rajput *jati* of Lohtamia of western Bihar or of Gamharia mentioned in *VR* which became an important ruling family in Mithila.

The third category is that of forest tribes which includes 17 *jatis*. The list is an interesting combination of textual material and local identities. For example, while the communities living in the jungles such as Koch, Kirat, Khas, Gond Nat, Pahalia, or Bahelia, Donwar and Bhatar can be identified even today in and around Mithila, others like Bhils, Pulind, Savara and Mlechha have been drawn from Sanskrit texts. These are not to be found anywhere in and around Mithila. Of these communities, of particular interest is the community called Kirata. In Sanskrit literature, kirata has been used both in the sense of a generic category, as a community living everywhere in hills and forests, and also as a specific category of people, probably the Indo-Mongoloids living in the Himalayas. It is in the latter sense that Bharvi in his celebrated work, *Kiratarjuniya Mahakavyam*, refers to the Kirata as the dominant community of the Himalayas, whose rulers commanded respect. Suniti Kumar Chatterjee's *Kirat Janakirti* focuses on the notion of Kirata in respect of the communities of the north-east, who founded the states and built up an impressive cultural system, drawing upon the then existing network of communication with the rest of the country. Recently, the Kirata has been described as a construct of Aryan discourse, the perceptions of the Kirata changing over centuries. It has been increasingly used in Nepal and the adjoining areas to denote the autocthones, i.e. the more primitive group as distinguished from the later migrants, including the Tagadharis, other Mongoloid groups and untouchables in Nepal. An essentially Sanskrit concept, the term is now used to denote a non-Sanskrit or even anti-Sanskrit identity. Similarly, it should be noted that the term *mlechcha* did not always denote an alien or a foreigner, or was always rigid and contemptuous in its application. It was applicable to both foreign and indigenous tribal communities, and was flexible and accommodating in its application, resulting in the absorption of alien communities in Indian society.

There is a category of communities which is supposed to serve the ruler. This includes the trading classes, business groups, cultivators and the service castes—almost all clean classes. Finally, the author refers to a number of communities engaged in begging or in criminal activities, known as the lumpen elements today, which were perceived as a menace to the city dwellers in those days. The description of women and the eroticism of *VR* will not go down well with present-day feminists who see evidence of gender discrimination. Further, the description of various classes of women such as *nayika, khangi, veshya* (prostitutes), *nagri* (artful women), *kulini* (old, haggard pimps) will be considered derogatory. Women were considered lower in status, *kulinism* further degraded the status of women.

It is said that *VR* projects essentially the view of a society composed of what is now described as Hindu communities. There is no reference to the Yavanas or Muslims or Islam. In fact, Tirhut or Mithila had already felt the impact of Persian culture, some elements of which were absorbed by Mithila society. For example, there are as many as 20 Arabic and Persian words in *VR*. My attention has been drawn to a *jati* called Tuluk included in the list of *mand jatis*. According to some scholars, Tuluk is none other but Turk. This raises various problems including one about the absorption and ranking of Turks within the category of *mand jatis*. At present, Muslim communities do figure in the local hierarchy of *jatis* or communities in different parts of the country. In fact, the Muslim is recognized as a 'caste' in a limited sense. But was it possible to do so in the fourteenth century when Turkish influence was barely 100 to 150 years old? There is evidence that the Muslims had settled down in north Bihar and were employed by the local Hindu chiefs in the same way as Hindus were employed by Muslim rulers. Therefore, was it possible for the Turk to be mentioned as a *mand jati* in the local hierarchy? This question needs to be probed further.

VR ignores the far-reaching changes in lifestyle occurring not only in Mithila but elsewhere too. The countervailing picture is provided in *Sharaf Namah-i-Mameri*, a lexicographical work by Ibrahim Qawwam Faruqi, who had migrated from Bihar to Bengal. This work also describes items of food and drink, clothes and costumes, utensils, games, etc., introduced by the Muslims. Alongside are mentioned the new classes of professionals which emerged: *Bazargan* (merchant), *Bazigar* (juggler), *Roshanhaz* (rope dancer), *Jamabaf* (weaver), *Sarraf* (money changer), *Zargar* (goldsmith), *Najjar* (carpenter), *Karra* (barber), etc. This issue is also linked up with the confrontation of cultures during the period under review. When Islam spread to this part of the country, as the Turko-Afghan rule was established, the existing society reacted in three ways. First, in the initial phase, as Vidyapati mentions in *Kirtilata*, the brahmans were harassed. There is evidence that a Chero chief killed the son of a Sufi saint. Second, a segment of Hindu society withdrew within itself and reinforced the norms of orthodoxy as part of a self-defensive strategy. Some of the works of Mithila of this period including *VR* could be cited as evidence of this, alongside the works of Goswami Tulsidas which simply ignores the presence of the others. Third, as the situation stabilized, there developed a better understanding of each other. Evidence of this is provided by the fact that the Hindu rulers reconstructed mosques or endowed Muslim shrines or employed Muslims who had brought in a new technology. A syncretic process was set in motion whereby elements of Hinduism and Islamic Sufism were sought to be fused. Kabir, living in the neighbourhood of Mithila, speaks at one level of the Hindu and Turk as separate ethnic categories with different religious symbols, *mandir* and *masjid* and extols at another level the underlying unity of all in terms of spirituality or *ruhaniyat*, oneness of god, and of values extending beyond the barriers of caste and creeds.

A comparison of the list of *jatis* given in *VR* and the list of *jatis* generated by colonial and post-colonial ethnography suggests that while a number of communities can be identified, there are quite a few others which could not be identified. The communities mentioned in *VR* have survived today either as a whole or as a subcaste or as a segment of other communities. Many communities have moved up the social and economic ladder. For example, Donwar which is mentioned as a forest dwelling community is now a segment of the Bhumihar Brahman and Rajput *jatis* and has acquired a new respectability. The Dhanuk, described as hillmen, fowlers and hunters, were later absorbed into the feudal system as housekeepers or domestic help.

A related question that arises in connection with the interpretation of this work is whether *VR* constitutes a model of brahmanical orthodoxy. There is no doubt that this work projects a brahmanical view of hierarchy where some segments are looked down upon and even held in contempt. However, a broader view of the culture and society of Mithila during the medieval period is needed before passing any judgement. It would be a gross oversimplification to say that Mithila was only a centre of brahmanical orthodoxy. In fact, Mithila was marked by the convergence of various streams of thought and culture. Even within the brahmanical system there existed among authors of *smritis* a fairly wide spectrum of views, including even a pragmatic and somewhat liberal understanding of social issues. One of them recognized the right of the shudras to make gifts, or sell meat. Others of this period recognized the acceptance by brahmans of uncooked food and even cooked food from the shudras in times of distress. As mentioned earlier, the category of *mand jatis* was a heterogeneous one consisting of what may be described today both clean and non-clean castes.

Mithila was a centre not only of orthodoxy but also of heterodoxy in the past, and of *tantra* and *shakti* worship during the period under study. This explains the prevalence of non-vegetarianism among the brahmans and in the brahmanical system of this region. Some of the heterodoxic aspects of traditions survive in Mithila's folklores and folk rituals. The Lorik ballads and Dosadh's Salhes deserve to be studied as alternative paradigms. *VR* mentions only the *shastric* forms of marriage and omits the *asurik* forms of marriage. Vidyapati, however, describes the *lokik* forms of marriage rituals particularly those of the *Kohavar*. The *Kohavar* rituals deserve to be studied in depth because they are mediated by women who define their space and autonomy and subtly assert their identity and even dominance. The *Kohavar* rituals also symbolize induction into marital sexuality. There are many other 'irreverent' aspects of folk rituals including the rain-making rituals as also of folklores which are a vibrant part of people's consciousness.

Therefore, the picture of Mithila or of the country that emerges from an ethnographic study of *VR* is one of diversities of all types, ecological, social and cultural, standing at the centre of currents and cross-currents of political and even of market forces. It shows Mithila or even the whole country as a land inhabited by many communities. In fact, all regions of India have been a macrocosm of many influences, perceptions and identities. This, in fact, has been the essence of the Indian experience, and of the process of change and development in the country. Again, compared to Mithila of the fourteenth century, present-day Mithila, culturally rich but economically backward and impoverished, has been the centre of radical social transformation, with the *mand jatis* in the forefront, contributing what is Mithila's best known gift to the world of art, Mithila paintings.

APPENDIX

List of Communities/Segments (201)
Varna Ratnakara

1. *Manda—Jatiya*

Nagala, Tongal (Gangol), Tapasi, Teli, Tivara, Turia (Turi), Tuluka, Turikatara, Dheola, Dhangala (Dhangar), Dhakala, Dhanuk (hillmen, archers and flowers), Dhoara, Dhuniya, Dhalikara (door-keeper), Domva (Dom), Dovatarua, Khangi (Khangar), Sagaara, Hadia, Dhadhi, Bhala, Chandaara, Chamaara, Gontha, Ganthi, Gonti, Goara, Cavara, Oda, Sundi, Sawa, Panchakavara, Pataniya, Parigaha, Chawi, Mundawari (Mundari-dapper or Mund-barber), Vonda, Kadava, Nagara (40).

2. *Criminal Tribes*

Lobhi, Lavala, Laptora, Nanda, Narjih, Lampaka, Chora (thief), Chanchal (cunning fellow), Juara, Chhinara (libertine), Lagavara, Petakata (pinch-bellied), Naakata (with nose cleft), Kanakata (earless) (14).

3. *Vanik Putran or Trading Castes*
Sadhu, Swadhyayik, Sanuvah, Yashvahan, Bubudhi, Sayeyan, Sarath, Sinhala, Malakar, Gandhavanik, Ratnaparikshak, Velavar, Vaman (13).

4. *Castes Attending on the Ruler*
Goar, Vari, Vanik, Bauria, Kanwar (Kalwar), Mukhia, Varitha, Choragah, Agahara, Koeri, Kurmi, Rajak (or Dhobi), Nau (13).

5. *Description of Forest (Van Varnan) and of Jati Dwelling in Forest (Vantar)*
Koch, Kirat, Kolha, Bhil, Khas, Pulind, Savara, Chhairanga, Mlechha, Gontha, Vot, Nat, Pahalia, Podh, Donwar, Sagar, Bhatar (all described as mlechcha) (17).

6. *Hill (Parvat) Dwelling Communities*
Gond, Patgond, Savàra, Kirata, Babbar, Bhil, Pukkam, Panchari, Medh, Mangar (10).

7. *Description of Rajputra Kula (Rajputra Kulvarnan)*
Somavansha, Suryavansha, Doda, Chausi, Chola, Sena, Pal, Yadav, Paamaar, Nand, Nikumbha, Pushpabhuti, Shrinagar, Arhaan, Gupjharjhar, Suruki, Shikhar, Bayekwar, Gaanahwar, Surwar, Meda, Mahar, Vat, Kool, Kachhawah, Vayesh, Karamba, Heyana, Chhevarak, Chhuriyoj, Bhond, Bhim, Vinha, Pundiriyan, Chauhan, Chhind, Chhikor, Chandel, Chanuki, Kanchiwala, Ranchkant, Mundaut, Vikaut, Gulahaut, Changal, Chhahela, Bhati, Mandatta, Sinhavirbhahma, Khati, Raghuvansh, Panihar, Surabhanch, Gumat, Gandhar, Vardhan, Vahhom, Vishishtha, Gutiya, Bhadra, Khursam, Vahattari, etc. (62).

8. *Beggars (Bhikari)*
Jaga, Jogi, Nagaari, Bharhar, Bhandua, Chenga, Chataria, Surtaria, Mahor, Goria, Vahili (11).

9. *Others*
Malakara, Gandhavanika, Ratnaparikshaka, Vanitapati, Supkara, Prasadhaka, Gandhakara, Manimarajna, Lipivachaka, Srutidhara, Sanstrajha, Vari, Varika, Kanvara, Jaga, Yogi, Nagari, Bharahara, Bhandaua, Chatariya, Surataiya, etc. (21).

REFERENCES

Abul, Fazl, *Ain-i-Akbari*, ed. Blochmann, Calcutta: Bibliotheca Indica, 1867-77.

Askari, S.H., 'Lexicographical Works of Medieval Bihar as Source Material for the Study of Contemporary Social History', in S.H. Askari and Qeyamuddin Ahmad, eds., *Comprehensive History of Bihar*, vol. II, part I, Appendix I, Patna: K.P. Jayaswal Research Institute, 1983, pp. 530–48.

Buchanan, Francis, *An Account of the District of Shahabad in 1812–13*, Patna: Bihar and Orissa Research Society, 1934, pp. 51–2.

——— *An Account of the District of Bhagalpur in 1810–11*, Patna: Bihar and Orissa Research Society, 1939, pp. 66–169.

——— *An Account of the District of Purnea in 1809–10*, Patna: Bihar and Orissa Research Society, 1928, pp. 58–155.

Chatterjee, Suniti Kumar and Babua Mishra, eds., *Varna Ratnakara of Jyotirisvara Kavi-sekharacharya*, Bibliotheca Indica, no. 262, Calcutta: Royal Asiatic Society of Bengal, 1940.

Chatterjee, Suniti Kumar, *Kirata Jana-Kriti: The Indo-Mongoloids: Their Contributions to the History and Culture of India*, Calcutta: Royal Asiatic Society of Bengal, 1951.

Choudhary, Radhakrishna, *Mithila in the Age of Vidyapati*, Varanasi: Chowkhamba Orientalia, 1976.

———, *History of Muslim Rule in Tirhut*, Varanasi: Chowkhamba Publication, 1970.

Gopal, Surendra and Hetukar Jha, 'Indtroduction', Bihar Volume, *People of India* (in press).

Jha, Hetukar, 'Varna-Ratnakara: A Social Survey', *The Journal of Bihar Research Society, Prof. Syed Hasan Ankari Felicitation Volume* (Special Issue), 1968.

——— 'Tradition of Urbanism in Bihar: A Sociological Probe', *Explorations*, vol. 2, 1–2 January–July 1988, pp. 47–55.

Majumdar, Biman Bihari, 'Vidyapati and His Age', in S.H. Askari and Qeyamuddin Ahmad, eds., *Comprehensive History of Bihar*, vol. II, part I, Appendix II, Patna: K.P. Jayaswal Research Institute, 1983, pp. 366–95.

Mishra, Anand and Gobind Jha, eds., *Varna-Ratnakar*, Patna: Maithili Academy, 1980.

Mishra, Yogendra, *History of Videha*, Patna: Janaki Prakashan, 1981.

Mukherjee, Prabhati, 'The Fate of the Autochthomous People', *Journal of the Indian Anthropological Society*, vol. 30, July 1995, pp. 109–13.

Parasher, Aloka, *Mlecchas in Early India*, New Delhi: Munshiram Manoharlal, 1991.

Sharma, R.S., 'Social and Economic Conditions', in B.P. Sinha, ed., *Comprehensive History of Bihar*, vol. 1, part II, Patna: K.P. Jayaswal Research Institute, 1974, pp. 359–73.

Singh, K.S., *People of India: An Introduction*, Calcutta: Anthropological Survey of India, 1992.

———, *Tribal Society in India: An Anthropo-Historical Perspective*, New Delhi: Manohar, 1985.

———, 'Tribal Medieval Bihar', in S.H. Askari and Qeyamuddin Ahmad, eds., *Comprehensive History of Bihar*, vol. II, part I, Patna: K.P. Jayaswal Research Institute, 1983, pp. 530–48.

Singh, Ram Deen, *Bihar Durpan* (in Hindi), 2nd edn., Patna: Khadga Vilas Press, 1888.

Index